Praise for the Book

"A heart-soaring book full of beautifully simple treasures to restore strength and serenity. A great book for anyone searching for balance and joy." **Deepak Chopra**

"Michelle artfully lays out the cure for the curse of the planet —low self-esteem—simply and lovingly."

Jerry Sears, author of "A Course in Miracles in 5 Minutes" and "Making Rain"

"I highly recommend this very special book to anyone who is ready to love life. It is a book you will joyfully read again and again."

Joyce Nelson Patenaude, Ph.D., author of "Too Tired to Keep Running, Too Scared to Stop"

"An essential companion for living with peace, personal potential and an appreciation of everyday greatness. This book is a treasure to keep for yourself and give as gifts for the people you care about."

Jana Stanfield, singer "Brave Faith CD" A motivational speaker

"The Cherished Self is a work of passion, vision and idealism. Few literary works today have these qualities. Michelle built a castle in the air, then provided us the wings to get to it. That is the beauty and brilliance of this work."

Belle Tuckerman, owner of The Belavi Institute

"The Cherished Self uncovers the subtle world that exists below surface existence, just waiting to be discovered and tapped by each individual soul. Once its influence is called forth into daily activity, a whole new mental and emotional reaction to life is established."

Rev. Dr. Michael Beckwith, Founder/Senior Minister Agape International Center of Truth

create a life

rich in love,

laughter and

simple pleasures

the Cherished Self

how to give back

to yourself

when you're living

a life that takes

all you've got

MICHELLE MORRIS • SPIEKER

THE CHERISHED SELF

The Cherished Self

How to give back to yourself
when you're living a life that takes all you've got

by Michelle Morris Spieker

The Cherished Self
31878 Del Obispo PMB #118-311
San Juan Capistrano, CA 92675
Visit us online at www.cherishedself.com

Editing: Robin Quinn
Cover design: Dunn and Associates
Front and back cover copy: Susan Kendrick
Interior book design: Natalie Sevilla

Printed in the United States

Publisher's Cataloging-in-Publication
(*Provided by Quality Books, Inc*)

Morris Spieker, Michelle
    The cherished self : how to give back to
yourself when you're living a life that takes all
you've got / Michelle Morris Spieker. — 1 st ed.
    p. cm.
    LCCN: 99-96057
    ISBN: 0-9673699-0-8

    1. Self-esteem in women. 2. Self-help
techniques. 3. Women—Psychology. I. Title.

BF697 .5.S46M67 2000   158.1
                      QB199-1342

Cherished Self books are available at special quantity discounts for bulk purchases for sales promotions, premiums, fund raising or educational use.

Dedication
This book is dedicated to the memory of Robert Hull.
It is a privilege to call you my friend.

Acknowledgments

I want to thank my beloved, Tom, for being who he is and for cherishing me eternally.

I am grateful to the following special people: my mother, LaJune Goss, for always believing in me and for having the courage to follow her own dreams; my father, Gene Morris, for always being inspired by life and for being a gifted writer; my sister, Marita Morris, for her encouragement and for guiding and protecting me through life. Thank you all for your constant love and support.

Thanks also goes to Diane Harmony for always being there for me. And to my friends: Diana and John Burge, Jena Leuenberger, Annette Mathews, Jill and Greg Lehr, Anne and Jack Kloenne, Gwyn Blanton, Aileen Menzies, Aggie Huff and Barbara Morris, I want to specially acknowledge that my life has been enhanced by your incredible gifts.

And finally, thank you Robin Quinn for your editorial magic.

the Cherished Self

Kathy—

Cherish yourself! soon—

Expect miracles because

you are one.

♡ Michelle Mont

Spielker

*A whole new you emerges once you make
the decision to cherish yourself*

CONTENTS

the Cherished Self

CONTENTS

the Cherished Self

CONTENTS

the Cherished Self

Foreword

A wish from my heart

If I had my way, I would wave a magic wand to plant a seed of self-appreciation into every person in the world. I would sprinkle the Cherished Self tools into the hands of every child and empower children to believe in themselves.

I would encourage authenticity. I would wish for the expression of the self, not society's idea of the self, but the real self. I would encourage diversity not conformity. I would teach that diversity is a positive sign. Individuals are born to express themselves.

I would pray for a world based on human connections, not just technological connections. I would ask for understanding to enrapture all of humankind. I would request that we learn to honor each other's differences and celebrate our similarities. I would pray to stop the painful wars that are caused by a lack of understanding of our differences.

I would hope that each individual could honor the entire human race and pray for the preservation of human life. I would pray for more love and peace to come into the world from one Cherished Self at a time.

It is up to you

My life transformed when I decided to cherish myself and then created the 15 steps to loving myself. I can look back now and say that the twists and turns of life that led me to this point all make sense. But I had a choice to make and so do you. I could have continued on the path of not loving myself and my life would have proceeded as a series of events and dramas to painfully awaken my soul. What I did instead was to make the decision to love and cherish myself and a whole new journey of life began.

I don't know what is happening in your life right now. If you are experiencing any level of pain, confusion, loss or crisis then my heart reaches out to you. I offer you the path of the Cherished Self. It is a glorious path of insights, deep connections, and discoveries of your true self.

Of course loving yourself is not the only answer to life's mysteries but it is one that will add a generous amount of joy, love and purpose to your journey.

It is up to you. No one else can make your journey for you. Remember there is only one you. And this is your chance to be true to yourself.

Introduction

I knew the ocean water had to be cold and the waves crashing on my skin must be stinging, but I couldn't feel anything. Instead I was numb—not from paralysis, from life.

As I stepped away from the water, I flashed back on my earlier years and wondered how I had managed to stray so far from my idea of happiness. Growing up in a small town in Nebraska, I had felt euphoric about living.

Naturally I set out into the world to contribute my unique part to make it a better place.

My goal was to create a meaningful life filled with love, purpose, good health and happiness. From that point on, I was in perpetual motion trying to build that life.

By my early 30's, things appeared to be in place. I had launched a successful career as an entrepreneur and marketing executive. I had married, acquired possessions, initiated a volunteerism plan to President Reagan, and maintained an active social life.

But somehow my attempt to live a good and meaningful life had led me astray. I began to feel an underlying restlessness. Largely ignoring the feeling, I interpreted it as a sign to push harder and succeed even more. I thought this was the way to achieve the life I wanted.

For a while I convinced myself that it was working. At least my life looked good from the outside. Inside, however, what was really happening was a departure from my real self.

It was at this juncture that my life took a major turn and I received some life-altering gifts. My marriage failed, my job in the film industry ended, and I discovered that I had exhausted my financial resources.

So there I was, standing along the water's edge looking out at the sea, feeling empty, exhausted and afraid of recreating the same life over again. I didn't want another 30 years to pass by only to end up at this same frightening point. Internally I had to ask myself where I had gone wrong. It became clear to me that my life had an element of smoke and mirrors. I had followed society's expectations as my guidepost for whether I was happy.

On the beach that day I realized I had been willing to do almost anything to hold onto my previous marriage because I was afraid that I was not lovable. I also recognized that I had become an overachieving pleaser in my career. Though I felt proud of my accomplishments, I knew in my heart that I kept raising the bar for productivity in the workplace to prove my value.

I wasn't sure exactly when I began to go astray from my real self, but I think it must have been very early in life. This desire to be lovable—to be valued and nurtured— had really become an undercurrent of my days.

Ironically this longing for love and appreciation had left me feeling unworthy, alone, lost and scared.

Reaching deep within myself, I somehow found a spark of hope. I began to make an inner plea: "Help. I don't know how to be happy. How do I live a truly meaningful life? How do I discover the real me? How do I live connected to my purpose? How do I find true love?

How do I not feel exhausted by the constant struggle of life?" The answer came from my inner voice and it said, "*Cherish yourself.*"

Though I immediately felt inspired by the answer, honestly I had no idea how to cherish myself. So I asked for guidance. I silently wondered, "What would it look like if every day I was cherishing myself?"

Eventually the answer came through meditation, journaling and time alone.

I began to develop what eventually became The 15 Steps of the Cherished Self. I was fortunate to have studied spiritual principles for years. I was also working closely with my own spiritual advisor. Using the insights and wisdom I had gained through these studies and my various life experiences, I created a strategy to learn how to cherish myself.

Now I know that learning how to love myself is the key element to living a meaningful life.

When I cherished myself, my life began to miraculously transform. With time, I welcomed real love, found inner peace, discovered the courage to be authentic, and decided to follow my passion of working in the field of personal empowerment.

At this point I felt inspired to call The Chopra Center for Well Being in San Diego to inquire about a possible position. For years I had been intrigued with the works of Dr. Deepak Chopra. Not only was I fascinated with his philosophies and spiritual laws but also impressed with his ability to touch and empower the lives of millions.

I was fortunate to have called at a time when they were looking for a marketing manager. Staying on the path of cherishing myself led me to an incredible opportunity to work for the Chopra Organization. Looking back, I can see that the experience of working there will forever positively influence my life. Not only was I working with exceptional people, I was also in a place where I could further generate the courage to follow my dreams.

I found fulfillment and great success in marketing the Chopra Organization. Yet while the environment was supportive, I found that I was falling back into my old patterns. I was losing touch with the many principles of cherishing myself. It was time to take a serious look at reapplying the 15 steps. Soon the 15 Steps of the Cherished Self were again an integral part of my life.

As time moved on, I saw how important cherishing yourself is in creating the life you want. I decided to share the steps with others. After a while, I made the decision to write this book and I left the job with Dr. Chopra. I spent the next year refining the steps and completing the manuscript.

So now I'm pleased to present the 15 steps to you through my book, *The Cherished Self*. These steps will be of benefit to you whether you're a career professional, a stay-at-home mom, a college student, or a teenager. The 15 steps work together to bring balance to the lives of all who are out of touch with who they are and what they want to create.

The 15 Steps of the Cherished Self are a charted path to your own self-discovery. They will provide insight and encourage you to be your authentic self. In the process of starting the steps, you will be confronted with a major life decision. Are you willing to believe you are *worth* cherishing?

If so, you will soon learn to see your life with clarity and discover the strength to become all you can be. You will learn to appreciate your inner core, and begin to listen to the music of your soul. Once you tune in with the truest part of yourself, you can then make the changes needed to live from your authentic self.

It is my hope that after you read *The Cherished Self*, you will feel an inner calling to be true to yourself. You will know how to love yourself daily and will have the tools to use every moment to be good to yourself. When you get caught up in the "busyness" of life, *The Cherished Self* can be a reminder that you can count on. And if it takes a while to get back on track, you will know that the 15 steps will be there for you to use when you're ready.

There is only one you. This is your chance to be true to yourself.

I wish you new powerful perceptions about life and yourself, and a true deep connection with the beauty of who you really are.

Here, take my hand. Come learn the ways of the Cherished Self.

Lovingly,

Michelle Morris Spieker
San Juan Capistrano, California

$$\boxed{\begin{array}{c} \hline 1 \\ \hline \end{array}}$$

Discovering Your Cherished Self

I'm going to ask you to make one of the greatest decisions of your life.

Are you worth being cherished?

The reason this question is so important is that cherishing yourself begins with the self-realization that you are worth cherishing. Cherishing yourself is an inside job. It begins with self-love.

In our society, we are not taught how to love ourselves. Instead we learn how to compete and strive to get ahead. And we are expected to give love to others and to be available for everyone else. On top of it all, we are even told "just love yourself more," despite the fact that we don't know how.

the cherished self

No wonder so many people feel depleted and lost. We're expected to accomplish an impossible task . . . to give and give to others something we don't know how to give to ourselves. *Love.*

Now what I'm describing is not an egotistical or boastful kind of self-love. Cherishing yourself does not mean you get to drop all your responsibilities, only be pampered, eat bonbons all day, and take never-ending bubble baths.

Instead, the kind of self-love I am referring to is a heartfelt connection that you can have with your unique essence. This type of self-love is the result of a subtle yet life-altering decision you make about yourself. It is knowing in your heart that you are worth cherishing.

Do you cherish yourself? *Only you know the answer.*

- Do you foster your inner glow?
- Do you feel a sense of connectedness to your purpose?
- Do you live out your days with a sense of calm and yet a heightened appreciation for the simple pleasures?
- Does life seem fair most of the time?
- Are you empowered to create your dreams?

When I had the courage and tools to love and cherish myself, I began to discover who I really was and then started to learn how to live in harmony with my true identity. I developed a strong sense of myself which in turn created a *whole* self. I came to know and nurture my Cherished Self.

When you cherish yourself, others will cherish you

My life shifted dramatically when I made a conscious choice to cherish myself. Still I can remember a time during a troubled past marriage when my husband used to ask me repeatedly, "What do you want?" I would often reply, "I just want you to cherish me."

I now look back and see I was missing a very important link in the process. I was asking him to cherish me at a time when I didn't know how to cherish myself. It was at that point that I realized I could no longer look outside myself for happiness. It was up to me and me alone.

I needed to learn how to connect with and cherish myself. Then and only then could I really experience true love. *If we look for love and approval outside of our own heart, especially when we do not love ourselves, we will perpetually experience life as difficult, disappointing, full of drama and confusing.* We may fail to ever really experience love, which is the greatest joy of life, if we deny ourselves the self-caring within our own heart.

When you cherish yourself, you cherish others

There are plenty of people who say to me, "Yeah, yeah, I need to love myself but it makes me feel awkward. Learning how to love myself seems self-indulgent. Shouldn't I be learning how to love and cherish others?"

The truth is that when we cherish ourselves, we cherish others. *The best way to learn to cherish someone is by learning to unconditionally love yourself.* Again, I'm not talking about an egotistical love. I'm referring to a self-love that enhances yourself as well as others.

I am reminded of the oxygen mask on an airplane. We are instructed to place the oxygen mask over our own nose and mouth first before helping a young child. This is to assure that we remain conscious so that we can be there for the child. In a similar way, when we only give to others and never replenish our own hearts, we begin to lack essential nourishment and become a depleted self. Thus we have less to give to those around us.

Qualities of a depleted self

A Depleted Self blames others for life's circumstances. A Depleted Self is exhausted. A Depleted Self is bored with life. A Depleted Self complains. A Depleted Self is resentful.

Qualities of a cherished self

A Cherished Self takes personal responsibilty for their circumstances. A Cherished Self is compassionate not only to self but to others. A Cherished Self is vibrant. A Cherished Self feels a connectedness to life and contributes their unique part.

A Cherished Self does not look to others to make them happy, secure or loved. A Cherished Self loves oneself.

The greatest decision . . . to cherish yourself

At first you may feel some resistance to the idea of deciding that you are *worth* being cherished. This is not unusual. This question touches our inner fears. If your initial reaction is resistance, give yourself some time to get comfortable with the idea. You may be thinking, "I know I want to do this but I don't know if I can" or "This idea seems awkward and embarrasses me." Whatever the voice is on the inside, acknowledge it. It's fear and that's in your way to loving yourself. It seems we are afraid of our own greatness, or afraid of failing, and sometimes we are afraid of being punished for loving ourselves.

Discovering Your Cherished Self

For me, cherishing myself became easier when I thought of some-one who I loved and cherished. I remembered my nieces and nephew and their irresistible spark for life. I recalled how dear they are to my heart and how a smile comes to me when I think of their cute faces. I have a natural tendency to protect them, love them, and encourage them.

The key to cherishing yourself is recognizing that you are valuable, lovable and definitely worth being cherished. Once you are ready to make this decision for yourself, you will discover an inner confidence that was trapped just behind your fears.

Be aware that there is a distinction between just *wanting* to cherish yourself and actually fully accepting that you are *worth* being cherished. When you accept in your heart that you are worth cherishing, from that moment forward your life is enhanced.

I believe that much of what our life presents to us is a direct reflection of how much we love ourselves. So if your life continually disappoints you or if you are unhappy, it's time to find out why.

It is time to say out loud, "I am worth being cherished!"

As easy or difficult as this decision is for you, what's important is that you do it.

Once you make this decision, the voice inside your head will become more self-affirming. You will start thinking such things as:
- "I value who I am."
- "I want to discover my gifts and develop them."
- "I want to have a stronger sense of myself."
- "I deserve respect."
- "I want to live in harmony with my true identity."

the cherished self

Leave the victim mentality behind

After I decided I was worth being cherished, an important shift occurred in my life: *I let go of being a victim.* This process began when I noticed times that I blamed others for my situation. I now realize that I was immobilized by my dilemma of focusing on the negativity in my life. I now see that I used to spend more time pondering why something bad was happening to me rather than solving how I was going to create a positive outcome. *Believing I was a victim made me feel powerless to change my life.*

Feeling like a victim to life's circumstances is one of the most debilitating experiences. Unfortunately the victim consciousness is rampant in our society. All we have to do is turn on one of the many talk shows and we will experience extreme cases of individuals yelling, screaming and blaming each other for their pain. People who refuse to take responsibility for creating their own lives spend their days blaming others for their misery.

A cherished self makes choices

When you accept that life does not happen to you but that you co-create your experiences, you let go of being a victim. This does not mean that uncomfortable, unfair or "bad" things won't happen to you, but you will know that you have a choice in how you handle life's circumstances. *You will see that you can make more responsible choices.* When you love yourself and know you deserve respect, then you have the power to create a respectful outcome from any twist or turn life may toss at you. Your Cherished Self is relying on a solid foundation . . . that you are worth being cherished. This knowingness creates a positive outpouring of energy in your life.

A cherished self experiences freedom

Knowing that you are worth being cherished and that you have choices in life gives you freedom. There is a great deal of energy and power drained from our lives when we feel victimized and powerless.

Once I was working with a client who was feeling completely unhappy and trapped. She was in an abusive relationship and could not see her way out. Then something magical happened. With encouragement, she decided that she was worth being cherished. As she started to take responsibility for creating her life, she experienced a transformation. Suddenly she was able to tell me, "I don't deserve this mistreatment and I'm not going to take it any more." The abusive relationship ended.

When you let go of blame, take responsibility for identifying the true cause of your problem, and honestly look at your reactions to circumstances, then you can take life-altering actions. You free yourself to create a cherished life.

The cherished self exercises
Cherished

Write down the words "I am worth being cherished" on brightly colored index cards. Next, place the cards in many areas where you will be able to see them throughout your day. Some locations might be on your refrigerator, on the bathroom mirror, in your purse, or in your car. Place five to ten cards in convenient locations.

the cherished self

Ending the blame game

Begin today to let go of blame. The first step is to start to notice times throughout your day when you felt like a victim. It could be that in your love life you always feel taken advantage of or you repeatedly seem to meet losers. At your job, you may feel unappreciated, underpaid, or unfulfilled. In a traffic jam you might think, "Just my luck to get behind the one stalled car!" Or waiting in line you may think to yourself, "I did have to pick the slowest line." Change your way of thinking and ask yourself, "How can I see myself making a new decision and taking action instead of feeling powerless to the behaviors of others?"

If you make even a small step toward feeling more responsible, you've made progress. As you make more changes, you will grow stronger and stronger and blame others less.

Even a Cherished Self will still face the same trials and tribulations that life brings to everyone. The difference will be that you won't feel like life is happening *to you*. You will take responsibility for your life and feel empowered to create a new experience.

2

See the Heart of the Matter

It's time to look at your life. I mean *really* look at your life. The true Cherished Self sees through to the heart of the matter.

It takes a lot of courage to see the truth. I believe that is why some people can go through an entire lifetime not being happy. People will stay in a job that denies them passion, or they remain in a relationship that depletes their vitality, or they become addicted to alcohol and are not willing to stop. *It takes real courage to live from your true spirit.*

the cherished self

In order to cherish yourself, you have to be willing to take an honest look at your life. You need to ask yourself some vital questions and truthfully evaluate what is going on. These questions include the ones listed below.

	Often	Sometimes	Never

"Am I happy?"
"Am I compromising myself?"
"Am I living my purpose?"
"Do I have joy in my life?"
"Am I blaming others?"
"Am I complaining?"
"Am I addicted?"
"Am I obsessed?"
"Am I controlling?"
"Do I feel stuck?"
"Am I overwhelmed?"
"Do I love myself?"
"Am I in balance?"
"Am I healthy?"
"Do I love my life?"
"Am I working too hard?"
"Am I not working hard enough?"
"Do I have loving relationships?"
"Do people like me?"
"Am I fun to be around?"
"Do I feel safe and supported?"

To look at your life is to observe your life. In this step, you want to see your life as though you had stepped outside of yourself and were looking back from nearby. You want to see without judgment and without regret. *Just observe and witness yourself.*

See the Heart of the Matter

I have discovered that seeing the heart of the matter is one of the most powerful tools in my life. I can do it at any moment. For instance, when I am walking around my house, I can observe myself as if I were my best friend and were perched on a balcony at a higher level. I take note if I look stressed, happy, hurried, peaceful, worried, confident, overwhelmed or content. Or, while I am working, I can observe myself interacting with associates.

Also, in moments of observation, I might choose to review a certain period of my life as if it were a movie. It is a good idea to get in the habit of reviewing the events of the day every evening before you go to sleep. Any and all matters of your life can be observed and witnessed from a new perspective, *outside yourself.*

Love notes to yourself

A special habit that I recommend is to write down observations of your day. I call these written observations, "love notes to yourself." Jotting quick notes to yourself will help you to identify what is really happening in your life. Your page may read, "I noticed I was stressed today. Why?" or "I am feeling joy. Why?" When you make little notes to yourself, you remind yourself of your experience. Reviewing this information allows you to stay in touch with your life and be the observer.

Why observe yourself from the outside?

There is a very good reason why you will benefit from taking a point of observation outside of yourself. This is where you can gain a new perspective on things. You will see your life as you see other people's lives. We often observe our friends, family or strangers and in many situations are able to see their lives clearly. For example, we recognize when someone is not happy, or looks tired, or does not have the zest they used to have. We think it is their job that is dragging them down, or that they have not been happy ever since they became involved in their current relationship. Or perhaps we notice that it is when they are playing their music that they are really enthused about life. We look, observe, and evaluate, and see what someone else needs to do. However, rarely do we look at our own lives with the same eyes. I believe that when we begin observing our lives from this new perspective, we place ourselves in a powerful position to begin making changes.

I can think of many examples in my life when I could not see my own sadness. Probably the most noticeable one relates to my first marriage. When I was involved in the troubled relationship I had no idea how really miserable I was on the inside. I disguised it by throwing myself into my career, creating an active social calendar, and convincing myself that I was happy. Looking back, I can now recognize that I was afraid to see the truth. Had I used the step of observation and witnessed myself from that new perspective, I would have been able to acknowledge the ways I was avoiding seeing the pain and could have begun making changes sooner.

Focusing all our attention on the lives of others can be a way to avoid looking at ourselves. This may be a bad habit that you need to break. Or you may just have never looked at your life in the same way that you view the lives of others. For these reasons and more, observing your life is likely to require a conscious decision.

As an observer, you can recognize the traps that hold you back

I believe that hardships often reveal that we are not paying attention. The art of observation involves seeing with honest eyes and looking for the authentic self.

When you aren't observing or being alert about your life, you can fall into unconscious traps. You may not even be aware that you are unhappy, are overworking, are obsessing about things, or rarely laugh. You might not recognize that you dislike your work because you have forgotten what it is like to be really happy. Or you may be vaguely conscious of your negative feelings, but have not acknowledged the depth of your pain and your lack of joy.

Some of us may overwork, over exercise or watch excessive television and not realize that can be as hurtful as an addiction to drugs or alcohol. Ultimately, we may lose touch with our families, our friends and our personal desires.

I know for myself there have been times when I looked back on my life and I wondered, "What was I thinking?" "Why did I even take that job?" "Why did I get involved in that relationship?" "Why did I buy that?" It was as if some part of me was not conscious and I stopped paying attention to my own happiness. When I began to observe my own life, I could see early on when I was heading for a situation that was not good for me. Observation helps us to take responsibility for our life and avoid the traps.

Thomas Moore, author of *Care of the Soul*, explains that when you observe yourself, you serve yourself. He points out that "serv" is part of the word "observance." And he states, "We can't care for the soul unless we are familiar with its ways. Observance means to watch out for but also to keep and honor. When people observe the ways in which the soul is manifesting itself, they are enriched rather than impoverished. They receive back what is theirs, the very thing they have assumed to be so horrible that it should be cut out and tossed away. When you regard the soul with an open mind, you begin to find the messages that lie within the illness, the corrections that can be found in remorse and other uncomfortable feelings, and the necessary changes requested by depression and anxiety."

Look for the answers

The Cherished Self will help you look boldly at the circumstances of your life, considering all matters to be of equal importance. Observe your life and notice what is bothering you, what is exciting you, and what is numbing you. *When you look at your life and courageously question it, you give yourself the ability to create a positive change.*

Though the step of observing yourself may appear to be simple and of minimal value, that is far from the truth. There is a life-altering distinction between allowing life to happen, and *being in charge.* When you feel empowered, you begin to see that you have choices. That there is a direct correlation between the choices you have made in the past and where you are today. *Choices you make today will predict your future.* Every aspect of life has value and gives us input. You can choose to be aware or you can choose to be blind to the choices that are available to you each moment.

There is a sense of vitality, power, strength and freedom that comes when you take on the responsibility of looking at your life. All of a sudden even the so-called insignificant events bring you joy, wonder, and most important, answers. *Who are you?* You notice changes in your body, in the way you talk, when you feel uncomfortable, and who you like or dislike. Observation gives you the ability to be able to peer into the future. Your life is giving you messages in every moment.

When my clients become willing to observe themselves and glean the gifts from their experiences, their lives transform magically. Here are some of the observations that my clients have shared with me.

Observation	Insights/Gifts
Why was I passed over for the promotion?	I don't know how to ask for what I want.
Why is there so much chaos in my life?	I feel bored when life is peaceful.
Why can't I meet a nice guy?	I'm really not ready for a relationship.
Why do I always have money problems?	I shop as a way to take my pain away.

Recently I watched a TV interview of the actress Sharon Stone. She was asked if she was always the beautiful, confident woman that she is today. She said, "No, as a matter a fact, I was a tomboy when I was growing up and extremely shy. Then one day I decided I wanted to re-create myself. So I purchased style magazines, watched confident people, and created the person I wanted to be."

When we observe our life we are able to make conscious choices to create what we want.

Be loving and do not judge yourself

The inclination is to judge and compare ourself to some outside standard. It is now time to set your own standards. Again, let me say that it takes a lot of courage to authentically live your life. Self-observation can be the tool that helps you become more real and true to yourself.

When you observe yourself, you risk feeling disappointed in what you see, or even more frightening, you may recognize a need to change an area of your life. If you don't look, then you don't have to accept responsibility for changing. However, it is not enough to just see something and realize it is time to change it. You want to also learn your lessons from it.

the cherished self

Observation is about seeing the gifts from every situation in your life, particularly the tough ones. *Observation is not simply about changing from one behavior to another; it is about gaining the lessons from your experience.*

We are quick to judge ourself when we realize we are in a bad relationship or the wrong career, or we spend a lot of money or we eat too much. This is where *cherishing yourself* plays a very important role. At these times you want to extend unconditional love to yourself. Learn to accept all parts of yourself: the good and the not-so-good. Keep observing what is happening in your life. When you notice something negative about yourself, ask: "What am I to learn from this observation about myself?" Every moment is giving us messages if we choose to hear them.

Sometimes it's okay not to look

Maybe you're not ready to look and that is okay! This is your journey and your experience. There is no perfect way to do life. But it's when the circumstances of life have you down and you're too afraid to look, for fear of change, that you get stuck.

It's important to recognize that different choices will bring different results. For example, if you sense that you are in the wrong relationship, you may not want to look at the situation. Observation might force you to leave that person, which may be too painful right now.

Life eventually will provide you with the clarity, strength, resources and time to do what you need to do. You are doing the best you can. Sometimes you don't like the life you have created, but you don't want to change. You don't want to lose something or someone. That is when you need to be gentle with yourself. Love yourself, be compassionate, and gain the gifts. No matter what the situation, gratitude will lift you and give you a fresh perspective. *Be grateful.*

Observation as a guiding light

If you don't look at your life, you will never realize how far you've come and won't know where you want to go. You can be on the course that you thought you wanted when you were 18 years of age and now, when you are 35 years old, you realize it doesn't feel right anymore. If you don't observe your life, you won't ask yourself, "Is this the right course for me?"

Whether you claim it or not, you are growing and unfolding in life. When you choose to observe your life, then you can use the information as a guiding light. This is a fast track to discovering your true self. You uncover your personal mysteries rapidly. You gain the lessons and you sharpen your perspective. As you begin to discover your true self, you know quickly when you are off course. You don't have to wallow as long in the process of learning life's lessons.

You are on the course of getting to know your true self, to ultimately living true to yourself. Self-observation will be a tool you use repeatedly on this life-transforming journey.

Write your eulogy

Here's an exercise that can be helpful when fear causes you to resist looking honestly at your life.

In 1994, I had a class assignment to write my own eulogy. I was told to write the eulogy as if I had died today. What would my family and friends say about me at the funeral? The assignment required that I write about all areas of my life: career, family, friends, my impact on society, etc.

This eye-opening experience riveted me to take charge of my life.

As I wrote the eulogy, I was immediately saddened because I realized that everyone who might speak at the funeral would talk primarily about my career. They all mentioned how driven I was in my work, commented on my entrepreneurial spirit, and said how much I loved my professional life. There were only brief remarks about me as a friend, a daughter and a family member, but mainly the service focused on my career contribution.

When I turned in my assignment, I felt so disappointed with my life. I realized I was not being true to myself.

The next week's assignment gave me the opportunity to create the life of my dreams. The teacher said, "Okay, you did not die yet, instead you lived three more years. And in these three years, you lived the life of your dreams. Go and rewrite your eulogy."

I was elated. This second eulogy was very different. This time, everyone who spoke mentioned my passion for being true to myself. They talked about my commitment to family and friends. They discussed my community involvement. They mentioned my desire to be there for my friends and family members in need.

They pointed out my joy in the simple pleasures of life. And there was little mention of my career.

In 1998, I found my eulogy assignment in a notebook and when I read it I had to cry for joy. I was now living the life of my dreams!

For me, writing these eulogies gave me the ability to look at my life from a view outside myself and I was able to make changes.

I now encourage you to write your own eulogy.
Create two versions:
1. As if you died today
2. As if you lived three more years and created the life of your dreams

3

Time for Silence

The most precious key to opening the golden door to your authentic self is to discover silence and the ability to delve into your inner essence. *This is where you will meet yourself.* In the silence, you will discover the vastness of your inner being. You will revel in the sweet music of your soul. This is your private time to be with yourself. You will access the miracle of who you are and rejoice in the unique combination of experience, spirit and personality that only you bring to this world.

the cherished self

We are comprised of two aspects:
inner self and outer self

Life is about living from both the outer and inner parts of yourself. Your external life is comprised of what you do. This includes how you look, how you relate, what you own, where you work, what you say, and how you act. Longings such as greed, power and prestige are aspects of the Outer Self also known as the ego. From your Inner Self, you gain perspective, guidance and joy. You can experience and create your true life through this internal part. There is a delicate balance between these two aspects of yourself.

Silence is the gateway through which you discover your Inner Self and who you are. To give your life harmony, you must access this inner part of yourself, while also having a full external life.

By entering into your inner silence, you will be able to quiet your mind and tap into the wealth of information stored within your being. Not only will you gain new insightful internal clues but you will also be able to reflect on your outer experiences of life. When you are still and enter the silence within, you will be able to learn to detach from the experiences in your life. This will give you greater insight and guidance.

If you avoid your Inner Self and only focus on the outer aspects of your life, signals will start showing up to get you to pay attention. These signals rise to the surface in the form of stress, disease, anxiety or discomfort. And if you continue to avoid your Inner Self, you may lose perspective, become materialistic, and greedy, choose the wrong partner, and look outside yourself for your worth. Placing a disproportionate amount of importance on things that have little to do with who you really are will cause you to feel tired and unfulfilled. By thinking, "If only I had more money or a relationship then I would be happy," you may become an exclusively "outer referral" being.

Your body does not have the ability to replenish and gain valuable guidance when you choose to look outside yourself for all your answers. You're just busy doing, doing, doing. Yet by turning to the inner aspect of yourself and resting in the vastness and the stillness found there, you will be able to recharge, gain a sense of peace, and feel guided.

When you go to your internal stillness, you can ask questions and receive your own answers. I'm not talking about society's answers or your best guesses, but your *authentic answers.* The journey of *The Cherished Self* is about discovering and living by your own inner personal truth.

It takes discipline to be still

We live in a society that is busy and demanding. Our jobs, our families, our friends, our communities, and our responsibilities are all pulling at us and placing expectations upon us. There is barely enough time to get everything done, let alone have a little fun. So when do we have time to be still and go into the silence? The reality is that we must somehow find the time, especially when we are the busiest. That is the irony. *What the silence does for you is center your thoughts and lets you know when you are off your path.* Silence empowers you to get it all done . . . with joy and peace. Go ahead and try it and you will notice an overwhelming sense of peace and clarity in your life.

The Cherished Self sees and values the silence. When you are cherishing yourself, there is nothing that becomes more important than honoring the inner part of the soul and listening to its guidance. You begin to awaken to who you are and how you uniquely contribute to the overall scheme of life around you.

the cherished self

On visiting your inner world

What is it like to be in the silence? I experience it as a sense of calm. A quietness. A sense of surrender. A feeling of connectedness. Even if I am not able to tap the silence, I still feel renewed and inspired when I become still. There is no such thing as an unsuccessful attempt to meditate. To cherish yourself is to allow every thought to occur and then let it pass.

When you are trying to get to the stillness, you don't want to punish yourself for having thoughts, eventually the thoughts will quiet and the stillness will emerge between the thoughts.

When I first started going into the silence through meditation, I felt awkward and uncomfortable. I had so many thoughts running through my head that I became frustrated with the idea of trying to still my mind. I would stop almost immediately and say, "This is just not for me!"

Then I kept hearing about the incredible miracles that were occurring in the lives of people who meditate. I heard of people who reduced stress, found clarity, and even healed themselves of terminal illness because of meditation. I decided it must be worth trying a few times. Yet the frustration mounted over and over again.

Later I discovered that my greatest successes with meditation came when I was in a meditation group or if I listened to a guided meditation tape. So, in the beginning, that is exactly what I did. I joined a meditation group in my area and I purchased several guided meditation audio cassettes.

Eventually I developed the ability to have a successful meditation alone. Today I meditate on a regular basis by myself. I find I enjoy going into the silence so much that if a client is late, or if I have to wait in a line, I take the opportunity to quiet my thoughts and enter the world of silence even in the midst of a busy day.

How to reach your inner silence

It's important that you learn your own technique for going into the silence. Some people take a meditation class. Others practice and develop their own way based on advice they find in books and elsewhere. There is not a right way to enter the silence, there is just your way.

Here's one approach I use. First, in your mind, turn down the outside noise. Get comfortable and close your eyes. Now quiet the chatter inside your head.

Let go of your thoughts. Watch them go by and then let them go. Now breathe, and with each breath, let go of your thoughts. Continue breathing and letting go of your thoughts.

It is the emptiness between your thoughts that is your inner silence. When a thought occurs in your mind, watch the thought pass through and let it go. I pretend the thought is a bubble and I watch it go by or I might see the thought as a cloud in the sky and watch it float away without any attachment. *Get to the emptiness between your thoughts.*

When you reach that space, you have arrived at the world of silence. Don't judge yourself. You are doing great! As you get used to going into the silence, you will become more and more comfortable being there. Eventually you will be able to reach a blissful state even when there is noise and activity in the background.

So be patient. And when you reach your inner silence:

Just be. Most of us find that the act of *being* is difficult. We want to be *doing something*. While in meditation, it is the action of *being* that is your job. Rest. Let go of your thoughts. Relax within the magnificence of your Inner Self.

Ask your Inner Self questions. While in the silence, ask questions. They can be related to any aspect of your life. *You will receive answers.* An answer may come in the form of an inspiration to take a certain action or as a direct one-line answer. It may come immediately or it may appear later, but you will get an answer.

Always give gratitude. While in the silence, give thanks for your life. Even difficult experiences are bringing you new life lessons as you move closer to being your true self, *so always give thanks even for the painful things.* Gratitude opens up the possibilities and lifts your spirit to see the gifts.

Now that I regularly visit my inner silence through meditation, my life has more peace. I experience more clarity and am more creative. I feel strongly connected to who I am. If I begin to feel out of sorts, I immediately know I need to meditate. It also allows me to remain in detachment to the outer world in my daily living. Through the practice of remaining detached from my thoughts, I am able to gain greater insight and peace.

Dr. Deepak Chopra says, "Meditation is the greatest gift one can give themselves in a lifetime."*I agree.*

4

Reclaim Your Authentic Self

Life becomes magical when you discover who you really are and then find the courage to be true to yourself. It is rare to meet someone today who is being true to who they are, experiencing genuine happiness, and living their dreams.

Inside of you is a dream, a passion, or an idea. You owe it to yourself and to all of us to express your authentic self. Allow the music of your soul to be heard and felt. There is a seed inside of you that requires nurturing like any seed. Tend to its development, and it will grow and then blossom into your unique expression.

Let go and trust. Trust your heart and stay true to who you are.

the cherished self

Dance to the beat of your own heart

I love meeting someone who is living their dreams and expressing their uniqueness. I smile from within and silently congratulate their conviction to be their authentic self. Every person who is living their dreams gives the rest of us hope.

When I think of people who are living their dreams, I can't help but remember a special couple, Bill and Colleen. When I met Bill and Colleen, they were working in management for a construction company. They were both putting in long days and even working weekends.

When we would get together for dinner, there would be talk about Bill and Colleen wanting a different lifestyle and career. However they were not sure when and if they could ever leave their jobs.

Then one day I received a phone call. Bill and Colleen were both on the line. Colleen announced excitedly, "We're doing it! We've decided to take a six month leave of absence from the company. We've purchased a camper and we're going for a trip around the U.S." Cheerfully Colleen added, "We're going to go and enjoy life! Maybe while we're gone, we'll decide what we want to do with the rest of our lives."

I had the privilege of meeting up with Bill and Colleen during their trip; it was a treat! They were both relaxed, fun to be around and enthused about life. They told me that they had decided they were going to be moving to Austin, Texas to buy and restore homes. The last time I spoke with them, they were loving life.

Their courage continues to inspire everyone who knows them.

For each one of us, there is a different idea of living an authentic life. For some it may be working in corporate America. For others, it's being a stay-at-home parent. Yet for others, it's leaving the 9 to 5 world behind, and starting their own business. The paths are endless. There is an authentic beat to your heart, and you can learn to dance in sync with it.

The path of the authentic self

To discover your path, I recommend that you take an honest look at your life and peer into your heart. Explore what makes you happy and don't let society's expectations cloud your view.

As a society, it's being on the path to promotions, more money, more status and of course, power that we applaud. Being your authentic self may mean you're a trail blazer and that can be lonely.

Though I've never been happier, more at peace, or more content with my life than I am today, I still slip into wanting to live up to the societal ideal of earning a luxurious paycheck, having an impressive title, and being in the middle of the action.

But, for me, not being true to my authentic self is too high of a cost to pay to get a few passing strokes in life. When I was not in touch with who I am or what's important to me, I found myself trying to fit into an overwhelming framework of not only corporate values but personal values that I did not create. It was slowly eating away at me. I had to find my own way.

I want you to know that discovering your authentic path in life will not happen over night. There will be a process of self-renewal, of beginning to see yourself with a different set of eyes, and of developing courage. With time, connecting with your authentic self will become easier and easier. Eventually you will be able to chart a path that fits who you really are.

Renewal, a challenging process

Self-renewal can feel somewhat like a total renovation. You have to deconstruct the old ideas of yourself and you may think your life is falling apart. Just know that you are in the construction phase and soon this phase will pass. What will emerge is your authentic self.

Renewal was difficult for me because I had become so dependent on my career and its related accomplishments and social ties for validation as a worthwhile human being. I felt vulnerable and even somewhat like a failure when these aspects of my life began to have less importance.

I'll never forget going to a dinner party with friends when I was in the midst of shedding my old corporate image. I felt vulnerable and less interesting to people when I didn't have a fancy title or a high profile project I could discuss. The whole evening was awkward and sad for me.

The next day as I reviewed the feelings I had the night before, I realized how dependent I had become on my career. I had unconsciously been using my career identity as a way to relate to people, but I had not developed my authentic inner self. As the real me emerged, I felt lost and shy. Yet over time I was able to feel comfortable as my true self.

The process of discovering my authentic self began with identifying what was really important to me. I started by asking myself, "What do I truly value in life?" And at the core of it all, "Who am I, really?"

Steps to renewal

I recovered my authentic self through the process of renewal. This involved thinking about times in my life when I was really happy and about my values. For instance:

- I thought about times when I felt healthy, joyful, full of vitality and content.
- I remembered times when there was an innocence to my idealism about human beings.
- I saw myself as someone who required little in order to be happy.
- I recognized that I value relationships.
- I value having a loving healthy relationship with my partner.
- I value family and friends.
- I value my health.
- I value freedom.
- I value sharing personal triumphs and even tragedies.
- I value living my dreams and helping others to live theirs.

Take some time to consider what makes you happy and what you value in life.

Before I became my authentic self, life seemed difficult

Prior to renewal, I was in constant motion trying to be something different than who I really am. I was out of touch with my feelings and didn't know how unhappy I was at that time. I thought this was how it is done. I believed that I just needed to find the right career. That a career would not only give me prestige but also enough money so that I could live in the right neighborhood, drive the "power" car, dress in designer clothes, and find the right relationship. Then I would be happy.

I didn't realize that I was digging a big hole for myself. The more I *tried* to succeed at life, the deeper that hole became. I was accomplishing more success, granted more responsibility, and gained more prestige in my career. But it was also turning out to be increasingly difficult to consider doing something else. I purchased an expensive car, designer clothes, etc., and went into debt. As time passed, I was going further and further away from myself. At some point, I switched from trying to succeed in life to trying to stay ahead in life.

As the plot initially thickened, the key thing to me was not letting anyone know how miserable I was on the inside. Eventually I fell into denial. I became totally out of touch with who I was and who I was becoming.

An unexpected boost

I was in my late 20's living and working in Los Angeles when I began getting indications I couldn't ignore that I was living disconnected to my true self.

My body was starting to display signs of inner discontent; I was having chronic back pain and debilitating spasms. My doctor ordered me to have complete bed rest for ten days.

While I was lying down, silent and motionless, my mind began to reveal to me how miserable I was on the inside. My emotions swung like a pendulum between feeling a sense of accomplishment and a soul level disappointment with myself. I had an internal sense that I had gone off course but thought I was too far engrossed in my life to change direction. I felt like I climbed the highest mountain and was exhausted. My fatigue was compounded by the sudden sadness of realizing that the mountain I had climbed was possibly the wrong choice for me.

Then the phone rang.

A familiar voice said, "I missed seeing your smile today and heard you were out sick. I called to hear how you are feeling. This is Ronald Reagan."

I was in shock and disbelief. I shook my head thinking this must be a dream. But it wasn't. I was talking to former president Ronald Reagan.

My only previous connection to the former president was an exchange of greetings each morning. At the time, we were both working in the same office building in Century City, California. We would usually see each other in the lobby at the start of the workday. Reagan had just left office around this time and was in Southern California working at the Ronald Reagan Foundation. I was the concierge/ event planner for the building.

The former president interrupted my thoughts. "How are you doing?" he inquired.

Without hesitation, I boldly responded, "Not very well. And it's not my sore back that is causing me the most pain, it's my life. It's my disappointment with myself. I feel I could be doing so much more to help make this world a better place. But I'm already exhausted living the life I have created. I think there must be several people who feel the way I do; who feel they have more to give and yet they're so tired keeping up with their current obligations. You know, I even think we could solve some of the world's problems if we figured out how to help people not feel so overwhelmed and depleted."

A surprised but gracious Reagan said, "Why don't you write down some of your thoughts and let's meet to discuss them after you are feeling better."

the cherished self

As I hung up the phone, I felt lifted and joyous. Later I was amazed by my openness with the former president.

But apparently Ronald Reagan appreciated my candor. Within a month, he and I met at his office. We had a quick photo taken together and I gave him a written summary of my ideas for a volunteerism program. Within a day, Reagan had drafted a letter of response. He hand-delivered it to me on his way out of the building that day. As he handed me the envelope, he said, "Personally, I would like to assist you in your quest."

Over the next couple of months, I launched a volunteerism program in the building. Reagan agreed to be a keynote speaker to promote volunteerism. He was also the annual keynote speaker for the following two years.

The self-awareness that I developed while I was ill was the beginning of my realization that I could not continue living as a depleted self. And my work on the volunteerism program gave me a glimpse of what it would be like if my work matched my authentic self. Looking back, I can see that Ronald Reagan's support at that critical time is one of the reasons I was later able to develop a life that reflected my authentic self. However it was a few years before I took action and found a new way of approaching my life that was true to who I am.

You don't have to wait before making changes. Start taking a look at your life today.

What is your idea of success?

I used to think that success meant making a lot of money, having an impressive career, and hobnobbing with the rich and famous. Today, all that seems empty. It's not that I believe one should be poor and not accomplish things. It's just that when these material aspirations outweigh true happiness, then it all seems empty.

Today my success is really being there for a family member or friend, appreciating life, following my dreams, and being ethical.

Review the last exercise, and then write in your journal about your ideas of success. What would a typical day look like if you were living a successful life? Where would you live? What would your hobbies be?

Be prepared for change

Everything changed when I came in touch with my authentic self. Many people who thought they knew me were surprised by my new habits. Even I was caught off guard by some of the changes and had to get used to them.

Career. I went from being an entrepreneurial business owner, loving client presentations and high profile deals to wanting to write a book and work with clients privately to help them cherish themselves. Working out of my home meant that I did not go into the office and at first I felt isolated. I was becoming more dependent on my partner not only for emotional support but also for financial support. This felt awkward and belittling. I also realized how much I measured myself against my productivity. I used to think that if I produced a lot of results then I deserved to be happy. And if I was not productive, then I felt disappointed with myself. So when my "to do list" grew shorter working from home, this felt strange. In the corporate world, I had started my day with a "to do list" that would fill a page.

Relationship. I experienced a major shift in my life when I began living from the inside out versus the outside in. I used to be interested in men who were not capable of *true* emotional connections and my relationships did not have the *kind of depth* which creates true love.

I experienced a shift in the kind of man I wanted in my life. I wanted a partner who would be available to the relationship and who valued authenticity.

When I met this man, I had numerous adjustments to make in my own thinking and certainly in my reactions. I must admit I was scared at first. It was hard to believe I could really trust him. I had to tell myself, "It's really good to feel this safe and happy."

Strangely, one of the hardest adjustments was in my own behavior. Let's just say the old me would do this unconscious thing, especially when I was around a man I was interested in. I would *try* to be funny, positive, sexy and interesting.

When I met an authentic man, I could no longer be inauthentic. This was a challenge. I was so conditioned to this old behavior that it took a while for me to trust that *the real me* was good enough.

The key for me was being prepared for changes. When the dust settled (and it did), what I was left with was my dream. I realized I could not be happier with my life but there was a period of adjustment. I had to let go of my attachment to my old ideas of success.

It takes courage

Somewhere inside of you is the strength to live your dreams . . . the conviction to be true to yourself. It all comes down to having "courage." *Courage is the propeller that keeps us pushing for what we truly want.* Courage says, "It is possible. Now let's keep moving. You can do it."

I see courage in many of my clients who are facing a challenging time in life. Courage and strength appear in the lives of many clients who are going through a move, an illness, a job loss, a divorce, or some other major crisis or change.

Courage may surface just as you're about to give up on a project. It could be that push you need to go and talk to a stranger. Courage shows up in our lives so we know that we are not alone.

Design a life that fits you

What would your life look like if you were being your authentic self every day? Design an authentic life for yourself and then begin to create it in the world.

Go for it! Begin with little steps and move to giant steps. One of the main reasons I wrote *The Cherished Self* is because it has been my dream to share this information with others. Though I sometimes thought to myself, "Who am I to write this book?" I surrendered and remembered that this is my dream. In fact, I've been passionate about it! *Following my dream fits my authentic self.*

the cherished self

Be your authentic self for a day

To discover who you really are, simply tap into your heart. Be yourself for a day . . . your real self. Do the things you love to do. Eat what you love to eat, wear the clothes you love, listen to the music you love, go to the places you love. Take in your experience. Then write your thoughts about that day in your journal.

5

Feel, Express and Grow

When you cherish yourself, you value feelings and recognize the need to access, express and process all the myriad of feelings and emotions that are going on inside of you every day. *You develop the capacity to give worth to feelings.* In contrast, a person who has not discovered legitimate ways to express feelings will act out in explosive and irrational ways or may become depressed and isolated.

All of us are damaged by unexpressed emotions

Every time we turn on our TV, we see examples of violence and rage. I believe one of the reasons violence is so prevalent in our society today is that people have not learned how to value and process their feelings. *Many of us discount our feelings; we bury ourselves in our jobs, passions, addictions and responsibilities.* I believe few people have developed paths to process their feelings successfully. All of us are damaged by unexpressed emotions.

The feelings that you discount and ignore will be stored inside of you and become your unconscious reactions to life. You may be angry, sick, depressed or addicted and not know what is causing your behavior.

When we are unsure of how to process our feelings, we tend to look outside for others to make us feel good and to numb the uncomfortableness on the inside. We look to others to fix our problems when many times we could be looking within to find the real cause. *We have to learn how to acknowledge and then live with our own feelings, whether they are pleasant or painful.*

Techniques such as observation and going into the silence can help us listen to and value our feelings and who we really are. The information we receive is our guiding light on the path to becoming our true selves and to being at peace with our life.

Negative feelings sometimes creep up on us and can become overpowering. This includes such feelings as guilt, anger, jealousy, hurt, anxiety, resentment, disappointment, shame or sadness. So, if you recognize that your feelings are calling for your attention at that point or earlier, what are you to do then?

First, remember that many answers exist within you and are just waiting for you to discover them. Our feelings guide us to our answers. And it has been my experience that one excellent way to process feelings is by journaling.

Journaling, telling it like it is

Journaling is the act of writing your thoughts and feelings down on paper.
Life is ever-changing, vivid, alive and full of diverse experiences. If
you have begun to observe your life and are going to the silence
inside yourself, you have discovered a vast world of information about
who you are and what you are feeling, experiencing and being.

*When you write your thoughts on paper, you can visually see who you are
and what is happening in your world.* It is as if you are documenting
your existence. Putting words down on paper is the manifestation
of a thought. Through journaling, you are empowered to digest
and understand your life. You are looking for clarity and for answers. You are purging all the emotions inside you.

Most days I carry a journal with me nearly all the time. I use
journaling as a way to immediately access my feelings. When I am
angry, I write all the feelings I am having about the situation or
person. I get all my feelings out and then, eventually, I am able to
move on to the other side of my anger. I also write down questions
that I am struggling with in my life, and then answer the questions
as if I were my guardian angel. I wonder what my guardian angel
would have to say about each situation. When I ask a question and
then search for the answers that my guardian angel would give, I
begin to discover the solutions that are truly for my highest and
best good.

In many situations, my journal has been a good friend to me. This
has been especially true in tough times like when I had to face my
failing marriage. I had very few places to turn to for answers. I
wanted desperately to know what to do. So I would write in my
journal to purge my sadness and to try to understand the situation.
I relied on my journal to be there for me at all times. There were

many nights when I would wake up and cry and not know where to reach for support. But when I would start writing in my journal, I would feel someone was there for me.

I knew I needed guidance and support, so I would write and write and write. And when it became clearer and clearer that the marriage needed to end, I felt terrified. So I would write all my fears about the marriage ending in my journal, and search for the strength to face those fears.

Some of the fears I jotted down in my journal included: "What if I never meet someone else?" "What if I am single the rest of my life?" "What if I don't meet someone until I'm well into my 40's and no longer have the option to have children?" "What if this is the happiest I'll ever be?" "Am I not trying hard enough to make the marriage work?" Though my marriage was failing, I was scared of being single and didn't want to go through the ups and downs of single life. I was scared of letting go of the marriage and didn't know if I could bear the pain of ending the relationship. I didn't want to be labeled a "divorced woman."

A place to turn

When unresolved questions about your life are nudging at you, turn to journaling.

Write down one question at a time. Close your eyes and imagine you are your guardian angel and know the answer to the question.

Begin writing. Allow yourself freedom to write whatever comes to your mind. Do not edit your words; allow them to flow.

Continue the process. Ask another question. Keep going until all of your questions are resolved.

Feel, Express and Grow

By journaling, I was eventually able to walk through each of my greatest fears. I wrote about the worst case scenarios and decided I *could* face each of them. Because of this experience, I use my journal at every turn in my life today to give me clarity, strength and understanding.

Journaling, a tool every person can use

Journaling is a tool that is readily accessible for your use. We all have times when we feel confused, blah, depressed or anxious and we can't seem to put a finger on what is bothering us. *Through the process of journaling, we can unravel our tangled feelings, access the source of our confusing behavior, and then take active steps to address the pain or discomfort.*

I wish that all children were taught the value of journaling and began to write about their feelings at an early age. We need to know how to write about our feelings as well as how to write about such subjects as history, geography, sports, art or music. People who can find ways to get in touch with their feelings are more balanced.

Journaling is a personal experience. When you write in your private journal, you are safe. No one is going to judge your writing skills or hold anything against you. Your journal is your private escape, and what you write is to be seen by your eyes only.

Throughout life, we must deal with our inner feelings, especially when we go through difficult times. You may be dealing with a painful family experience, the loss of a loved one, a troubled teen, the romantic blues, the aftermath of a crime, a disappointment with yourself, the loss of a job, or any number of experiences of life that challenge us.

the cherished self

It is vital that we have tools to process the feelings that arise throughout life. If we fail to develop such techniques, we are in danger of slipping into unhealthy behaviors. We may withdraw from society, have temper fits, start using drugs or alcohol, become depressed, eat more, eat less, or become overly consumed with a sport or a project. When we are not in touch with our feelings and do not acknowledge or express them, we search for something or somebody to numb our feelings or ease our pain.

When you are not afraid of your feelings and know how to access them, you are aware of what is happening inside you and you are more balanced. You are able to handle the difficult situations with more strength. You discover or recover who you really are and then express it.

The Real Power Is in Your Imagination

You are not your past, you are your future

Every moment you are becoming. This truth possesses life-altering power and grants you vast freedom.

You are never trapped by life, you are only trapped by your thoughts

Have you ever had an uninspiring job, unhealthy relationship, or barren bank account, and felt you had no options to change your situation? Have you ever wanted something and then concluded that you could never have it? At such times, you think you're crazy for wanting more. *You fall into the belief that you simply have to learn to accept your lot in life.*

You see yourself as trapped. You feel depressed, defeated, and lose your joy. Your life becomes a self-fulfilling prophecy.

There have been many times in my life when I felt trapped by my circumstances, whether it was staying in a job because I needed the steady income, remaining in my troubled marriage because of my fears of being alone, or being in debt. Then I discovered a simple tool to create the life of my dreams. And true miracles occurred in my life.

Your secret power

When you are cherishing yourself, you understand that you are responsible for creating the life you have right now. You realize that what you create is based upon what you observe, experience and believe. And as you come to recognize your part in manifesting your life, you begin to wonder, "What can I do to change it?"

Well, the answer is magical and fun. *The answer is to begin to fire up your imagination.*

By tapping the power of your imagination, you will discover the capacity to make the changes that will enhance your life.

Many people have heard the expression, "You are your thoughts, so be careful what you think." This is so true. *When you are looking at the life you presently have and are focusing all your thoughts on what you see now, you will create the same experience over and over and over again.* You will overlook the fact that you deserve more.

Move into your imagination

One of the best ways to cherish yourself is to discover new possibilities for your life through your imagination. Your imagination is amazingly powerful. *By using your imagination every day, as you look ahead to how you want your life to be, you can actually step into that life.* So it's extremely important to think each day about what you want. What will make you happy? What are your dreams?

As you begin to tap into your imagination, some tools covered in earlier chapters will be helpful. These tools are:

1. Observing your life
2. Going into the silence
3. Journaling your feelings

Here's how these tools will assist you. When you observe your life from a different view, you begin to *see* yourself. When you go into the silence, you are able to give yourself permission to discover who you really are. And journaling your feelings and desires will help you recognize what you want in your life. What makes your heart sing?

Don't limit yourself to what you think is possible. Remember, you are living from your imagination and *anything* is possible.

the cherished self

Let's create your dreams

Up to this point, the steps have begun preparing you to call forth your dreams. You are now ready to actually create a new experience. So let's get started by learning the five steps to living from your imagination and creating the life *you* want.

Five steps to creating the life you want
> 1. Think of your desires.
> 2. Dream a lot and use your imagination.
> 3. Believe it is possible.
> 4. Trust the process.
> 5. Be grateful.

Think of your desires
Write down your desires and stretch your mind when you think about what you want to create. Start writing an ongoing list in your journal. Note and observe the elements you would like to incorporate into your life. What traits in others would you like to emulate? *Let your imagination roam and explore.* Make a list of 100 possibilities as your desires.

Dream a lot and use your imagination
It is important that you see yourself being it, doing it, or having it. Close your eyes at any point and see yourself in the future reality. This is called visualization. Seeing yourself in various situations in your mind helps you activate your thoughts during the creative process.
For example:

- See yourself in a fulfilling relationship
- See yourself in a rewarding career
- See yourself as healthy
- See yourself in the body you desire
- See yourself as prosperous

Believe it is possible

It's important that you believe it is possible. This is key to manifesting your dreams. In your heart, you must truly believe that you deserve *whatever positive thing it is.* I call that "placing an order." It may help to think of life as a big mail order catalog. Then watch and see what good things life delivers. I believe you are desiring these things because it is possible for you to create good in your life.

Trust the process

When you want to create a new experience through imagination, it is important that you go through the steps listed. However, *there will come a time for you to let go and trust the process.* You do not want to become obsessed or attached to the outcome. If you have followed the above steps, then your job is done. Let life do the rest.

Be grateful

No matter what life has brought you, be grateful that you can create new experiences. You have the power within you to change your life. Your mind is a wonderful resource, for within it lives not only the power but also the opportunity to achieve your dreams.

Be careful what you think about

Since your thoughts create your reality, it makes sense to be careful about what you think. Be in charge of your thoughts and keep using your imagination in positive ways. You can turn the most ordinary moment into an extraordinary moment by tapping your imagination. It is available to you at every moment of your life.

Be careful not to focus on negative outcomes or negative aspects of others. Such thinking creates more negativity in your life. Think of a negative thought as a toxin or poison in your body. You would not take poison if someone handed it to you. So, do not think negative thoughts.

I realize it is difficult not to think negative thoughts, however when we make a conscious effort to think about positive possibilities and about connecting with each other in mutually rewarding ways, then our lives are lifted.

A personal example of using imagination

When I realized I wanted to create a healthy loving relationship in my life, I knew I needed to focus on the qualities I wanted, not the qualities I didn't want. So I made a list of the positive qualities I hoped to find in that special someone.

For example I listed:

- I deserve to have a partner who knows how to openly and lovingly communicate.
- I deserve to have a partner who loves and accepts me the way I am.
- I deserve to have a partner with good self-esteem.
- I deserve to have a partner who likes to plan our dreams together.
- I deserve to have a partner who loves family.
- I deserve to have a partner who supports my spiritual aspirations.
- I deserve to have a partner who likes to do fun activities.
- I deserve to have a partner who likes to snuggle on the couch.
- I deserve to have a partner who likes to give to others.

One day he showed up. He was all the things I wanted in a companion. But at first I wanted to push him away.

I was working at the time with my spiritual counselor and she helped me to see what I was doing.

The Real Power is in Your Imagination

Our conversation went something like this:

Counselor: "How is the relationship going?"

Me: "I've never felt so safe, comfortable or happy in my life."

Counselor: "That's great!"

Me: "But it's not going to work."

Counselor: "Why not? What reason do you think you might have for pushing love away?"

Me: "Because it would never last. We're just too different."

Counselor: "You wouldn't be trying to push away love because it feels *too* good, would you?"

A week would pass, and again we'd discuss the relationship:

Counselor: "Now, how do you feel when you're with him?"

Me (smiling): "I have never felt so wonderful in my life. I love spending time with him. (smile disappears) But I still don't believe it will last."

Counselor: "Michelle, he is a direct reflection of how much you love yourself. He will not leave you if you believe you deserve to be loved. The fact that you have attracted him into your life is good. This means you are loving yourself. Try to hang in there and see what happens."

Each week I would surrender a little more to allowing healthy love into my life. I eventually decided to marry this man, and I feel like the luckiest woman alive. I am so glad my counselor helped me to develop the strength to break an old pattern of not knowing I deserve to have a healthy loving relationship. *I now know I deserve love.*

the cherished self

Use your imagination as a way to escape

When you are at your job and you feel trapped, slip into your imagination and see yourself in the career of your choice. Whatever the circumstance is, see yourself in a different way. See what your heart desires. Look at your relationships, finances, body, or your home and see yourself living your heart's desire.

What could you be pushing away?

Is there something you know you want in life but when it shows up, you push it away? It is time to take an honest look at your heart and question if you are afraid of feeling good. This dynamic of pushing away or sabotaging good in your life can occur when you get a promotion, a new home, a new car, a new relationship or an inheritance. *Mysteriously, we unconsciously damage our new lot in life when we fail to know we are worthy of such good things.*

While on your journey to loving yourself, be prepared to allow joy into your life. The way I allow joy and good into my life when I'm feeling unworthy is:

- I search for other people who are allowing good in their life and I identify with them.
- I journal about my feelings.
- I do something nice for someone else.
- I breathe and tell myself I deserve to feel this good.
- I go and see my counselor and work through my fears.

The Cherished Self recognizes subtle tendencies that destroy the positive things in one's life, resists the urge, and declares,
"I deserve this good because . . . I love myself!"

Creating Life-Enhancing Relationships

The value of having someone in your life who believes in you is immeasurable.

A life-enhancing relationship is as rare as the most precious of stones. When I speak of a life- enhancing relationship, I'm referring to that person in your life, who above all else, believes in you. This could be a friend, a partner, a parent, an aunt or an uncle, a neighbor, a teacher or a mentor.

There have been studies of children who have remarkably overcome great obstacles to develop into productive adults. These children grew up with poverty and/or abuse, and possibly abandonment. There is one common theme in these success stories. There was at least one person in that child's life who said, "I believe in you." The studies also showed it did not have to be a parent or someone in the immediate family. These children were sometimes influenced by teachers, neighbors, friends, mentors or distant relatives.

The Cherished Self recognizes the value of having life-enhancing relationships. When I was not cherishing myself, I took these relationships for granted. This is painful to admit but I see now that there was a time when I was overly absorbed with myself. I did not value those people in my life who were as rare as a precious stone. Today I make a special effort to value my meaningful relationships. This has enriched my life. I value my partner, my true friends, my family and special others.

What is a life-enhancing relationship?

In a life-enhancing relationship, your potential is recognized and nurtured. Only the best is wished for you. You feel safe with this special person.

You trust. Having the confidence that you can trust a person is beyond describing. Trust is knowing that you can tell them anything and it will be kept in total confidence. Also, this person will not bring up your mistakes of the past. You are lovable even with a few blemishes from past experiences.

You feel safe with the truth. You know you have a life-enhancing relationship when that person tells you the very thing that you need to hear although no one else has the courage to say it. You are told the truth. And when you hear the truth, you don't feel criticized or judged. Instead you say, "Thank you."

You are heard. Sometimes all that we need is someone to talk to and then we feel better. We do not need advice or long debates over our situation. We just need to share our feelings. Your special person knows when to give an opinion and when to listen.

You feel supported. This person is not afraid of your pain . . . and will be there for you through life's difficult times. Your tears are not discouraged. You get a hug when you need it. You are not abandoned.

You feel revived. It could be a phone call, a card or time together which gives you renewed strength. A meaningful relationship uplifts you.

Meaningful relationships in my life

I realize now that I was blessed with an extraordinary mother. I can remember her telling me over and over, "I'm so proud of you. You can do anything you decide to do. Whatever you want, you can have." She would tell me how proud she was of me even when I failed at a project.

I'll never forget the day I received my SAT scores from the school counselor and my scores were terrible. Though I should have remembered that my mind tends to go blank during tests, I thought the scores were a true reflection of my abilities. From school, I phoned my mother and said, "Mom, I'm a failure." She responded, "Wait right there. I will be there in just a few minutes." And she left in the middle of a workday to come pick me up at school.

She took me for a long drive. At one point, she parked the car and turned to me. She said, "That piece of paper does not determine who you are or what you are capable of achieving in life. You are more than these scores and don't let anything in life ever label you."

She asked me to hand her my SAT score sheet. After I gave it to her, she tore it in little pieces. She said, "I love you and I believe in you. Nothing will ever get in the way of my believing in you."

I felt like a new person.

Now, as an adult, I realize she gave me one of the most incredible gifts in my life. *She believed in me.*

Today I realize a life-enhancing relationship is a treasure. I am fortunate to have special friends, a wonderful partner, and loving family members in my life. But there have been earlier times when I surrounded myself with people who were not always supportive and who I'd classify as toxic.

What is a toxic relationship?

We all have people in our life who deplete us. These could be our parents, partner, boss, friends or associates. *When you are in the presence of these toxic people, you feel taken for granted, judged, put down, anxious and defensive.* Another way to tell if you are in the presence of a toxic person is that your energy feels zapped.

Most "toxic" people are embittered because they have been disappointed by life. They have not been given positive support, or they have been abused and their pain controls them.

It's difficult to avoid having a few toxic friends, family members or associates in your life. But when you compromise and allow these unhealthy relationships to stifle what you could be, you deny yourself love. You become influenced by their thinking and wishes.

Creating Life Enhancing Relationships

I am not saying you should abandon all the "toxic" people that you know. I'm saying that it's important to be aware of who they are and to make sure you do not go to a "toxic" person for your support.

Once at a lecture a woman began to cry when I spoke about "toxic" people and the importance of not going to them for your support or encouragement. She spoke up and said that over ten years earlier a man broke up with her and told her it was because she was not "good enough" for him. She said, "I realized now that I believed him, and I have given him my power for the last ten years." She added that she still dreamt about him at night and in the dreams he continued to tell her she is not good enough.

Like most toxic people, this woman's former boyfriend was overly self-focused and unconcerned with her feelings. Instead of being diplomatic and a friend to her when they broke up, he was unnecessarily cruel.

Fortunately this woman had a breakthrough at the meeting. All of a sudden, she realized that she had allowed a "toxic" person to decide whether she was valuable or not. She declared that she was never again going to allow him to validate her worth.

You know you love yourself when you have healthy life-enhancing relationships

There is truth to the statement that what we attract is a reflection of how we feel about ourselves. If you look around to the people in your life and all you see are toxic relationships, then this is an opportunity to take an authentic look at yourself.

the cherished self

I knew I was loving myself when I began to attract healthy relationships into my life. Now I could not imagine being in a relationship with a toxic person. This pertains to all areas of my life: work, home, family, friends and associates.

Unconditional support

This topic reminds me of the best support I ever received from a friend. This was at the time my marriage was failing, I was miserable and I felt very little zest in life. Every Tuesday and Thursday morning, I would go walking with a friend. She knew that my marriage was not going well and that I was terrified of ending the relationship. She knew that I wanted to make it work and to give it all I had. She was also aware that I was not happy.

During this period, I worried that if I told my friends how miserable I was, they would insist that I leave the marriage, and if I did not leave, they would judge me. I was scared. I wanted to disguise my unhappiness and I preferred everyone see how happy I was. I felt trapped between both worlds. I did not want to end the relationship even though I knew it was not working. I was in the middle of a life process and it was unfolding as I needed it to unfold.

During one walk, my friend stopped me, looked me in the eyes, and said, "I am here for you. If you never leave him that is okay. I will never leave your side. And if you leave him, I will be there for you. If you leave him and then go back to him, I will never stop supporting you. I will be your friend through it all. I just want you to know I am here for you no matter what."

Now that is real support! This friend was truly providing a life-enhancing relationship. Her unconditional friendship eventually played an important role in my ability to leave a marriage that was not right for me.

Creating Life Enhancing Relationships

Be the love you seek

One of the best ways to attract life-enhancing relationships is to be there for others. Be all the qualities you want in those special people and you will attract that for yourself.

When you cherish yourself, you love yourself and cannot help but treat others with love and respect. Others will feel loved in your presence.

Who's in your life?

Look at the people in your life and determine which ones enhance you and which ones deplete you. Write two lists in your journal.

Enhances   Depletes

If you lack life-enhancing relationships, then look at your circle of acquaintances and think about relationships you might want to cultivate. Or this could be a signal to go and meet new people.

Consider exploring a new group, joining a gym, volunteering at a local charity, reaching out to new places and discovering some new life-enhancing relationships.

If you already have life-enhancing relationships, think of a special way to acknowledge them. You might write a note thanking them for being in your life. Tell them how meaningful they are to you.

the cherished self

Counselors and life coaches

Sometimes having life-enhancing relationships in one's life is not enough. These are the times when life derails us. We feel off track, confused and traumatized. We sense that a trained professional could give us the special help we need. Someone who recognizes why we derailed and can help us see what we need to do to get back on track.

A trained counselor or life coach can provide clarity, tools and an unemotional perspective on one's life. They know the answers are within you, so they refrain from giving advice but allow you to discover your own answers. They give you guidance, support and direction.

At certain points in my life, I have gained profound insights by going to a trained counselor. The counselor was able to guide me through the crisis or phase with understanding and love.

8

The Healing Power of Nature

In our hustle-bustle lives with so many expectations to meet, we often overlook one of the most precious gifts . . . nature. At times, we frantically look outside ourselves to people, books, jobs, etc., for answers, yet miss the miraculous blessings that nature can provide. However, the Cherished Self is more in touch. *Part of the experience of cherishing yourself is to awaken to the magnificence of nature and to enjoy it every day.*

Lost in the concrete jungle

Ironically, nature is everywhere, yet sometimes we are blind to its beauty and benefits. I call this "cement-itis." During a certain

the cherished self

period of my life, my days consisted of driving to work, getting caught in traffic, parking in an underground lot, working in a high-rise office building, living with recycled air, and then leaving when it was dark. My work hours were a blur of telephones, computers, fax machines, voice mail, impersonal meetings and zombie elevator rides.

Even though the beauty of nature was *still* within my reach, I was caught up in the day-to-day scramble for success. I failed to note the sun's brilliance, watch the flight or hear the songs of birds, and missed the enchantment of the flowers and trees.

I was blind to it all because of my obsession with climbing the corporate ladder.

Likewise, I see plenty of mothers who are lost in the "mommy jungle." Their lives consist of rushing to get the kids off to school, running to the grocery store, stopping on the way home to pick up the dance shoes, offering to watch the neighbor's children for an hour, taking a child to a doctor's appointment after lunch, and getting the kids to soccer practice. After making sure dinner is prepared, there's the meal, helping with homework, then the children are bathed and made ready for bed. Mothers barely have time for themselves, let alone to enjoy the beauty of nature.

There are so many jungles out there to get lost in today. The life of a student is packed with school work, hobbies and social functions. The life of senior citizens is filled with taking care of the grandchildren, meeting volunteer responsibilities, and being there for a friend in need.

Many of us do not stop to appreciate the beauty of nature.

Nature activities

List all the activities you enjoy doing in nature. Give the list to the life-enhancing people in your world and encourage them to support you in doing the activities on your list.

The simple pleasures of nature

When our busy lives cause us to ignore nature, we miss out on simple pleasures. We cut ourselves off from a source of vital energy. Partaking in the pleasures of nature is one of the nicest and simplest things we can do to renew ourselves on a daily basis. So enjoy the artistry of the clouds, listen to a flowing river, smell a rose, dangle your feet in a pond, or caress a leaf today.

The experience will touch your soul.

It may feel like you're stepping out of a fog when you begin to see the beauty that surrounds you. In learning to cherish yourself, it is vital to step outside of the fog of self-absorption or daily demands and take time to notice the magnificence of nature.

Yes, it's true that I operated within such a blinding fog for many years. Though I would drive to and from work along the ocean, many days I would not even notice the water, the waves crashing, the sky with the beautiful clouds, or even a dazzling sunset. I was consumed in my own little world of busy thoughts, demands and strategies.

the cherished self

Nature has a way of lifting our worries

When you cherish yourself, you know you can rely upon nature as a place to go to find serenity, beauty, peace and answers. Nature has a miraculous ability to lift us away from our troubles, to quiet our minds, and to inspire answers. Cherish yourself and learn to recognize the support that nature has to offer.

You could plant petunias in the garden, marvel at the flight of a butterfly, feel the grass between your toes, or listen to the purr of a cat. Suddenly your burdens will lighten.

When I walk along the ocean's edge, sit in the sand and listen to the waves, suddenly my troubles drift away. And when I return to my daily life, the concerns seem less intense. I am better able to cope with my challenges.

Nature reflects our ability to rebound from setbacks

When you connect with nature, you are able to see the ability of the natural world to rebound from seeming destruction. You notice the recovery that occurs after a forest fire, an earthquake, a tornado, or a heavy rainstorm. *You learn that you can rebuild your life after a crisis in much the same way as a forest eventually experiences regrowth after a fire.*

After one of my jobs ended unfairly, I can remember feeling lost, stripped of my place in the world. I didn't know how to fill my days if I was not at work. With time, my life began to evolve and I started to discover new and exciting things to do with my newfound freedom.

Later, I founded The Cherished Self, an organization that teaches, inspires and encourages individuals to live out their dreams.

The Healing Power of Nature

Learn to connect with nature

One way that I interact with nature is by going outside and reflecting upon my connection to the natural world. I sit in a park, gaze upon a flower, and think about how that flower is like me.

I notice that the flower started from a seed and has grown to become a unique expression. The flower does not struggle to be more than just a flower. It has roots that give it stability. If the flower is placed in the shade, it will shrivel up and die. If it is placed in too much sunlight, it will dry up and cease to live. If it is too crowded by other flowers, it will not survive. And if there are too many weeds around it, eventually it will be overtaken by them.

The parallels with my life are easily apparent.

- Am I nourishing myself so that I will survive and even thrive?
- Am I trying to change my unique gift?
- Do I have a solid foundation in my life or will a strong wind come and knock me down?
- Am I giving myself enough time to relax and replenish?
- Am I getting enough sunshine or am I trying to be too much to too many people?
- Am I being overshadowed by others and letting the weeds overwhelm me?
- Can I just be who I am and not try to be something other than myself?

Not seeing nature's beauty is equal to not seeing your own beauty or the beauty of others. Can you remember the last time you really looked in your eyes and connected with your own magnificence? Do you recognize the beauty in others and your connection to them?

Identify with nature

Find a potted plant and place it in front of you. Take your journal and begin writing about how this plant is like you.

Write what this plant needs to survive and thrive. How are you like the plant?

What do you need to thrive? List all the ways you know you need to be taking care of yourself.

What happens when you don't provide yourself with your basic needs?

Nature teaches us how to just be

In life, there appear to be very few places where we are given permission to just "be," except in nature. Nature teaches us that we can just "be" all the time!

Many of us overburden ourselves with the preoccupation of always doing, doing, doing. Rarely do we rest in the wondrous recognition of who we are.

Nature teaches us to surrender to life's cycles

In nature, we experience the gentle transition of the seasons. We feel the sadness of a fading pleasure as the brilliant autumn foliage begins to drop from the trees, and get caught up in the excitement of a new season with a fresh early snow fall or the beauty of spring flowers.

The Healing Power of Nature

Nature reminds us of the cycles of life. The cycle of birth and death. The joy of celebrating the new seasons of our own life from an infant crawling, to a first step, to grade school, high school, college graduation, marriage, birth, loss and birth again.

When we feel the warmth of the sun, a refreshing cool breeze, or the chill of a storm, we are lifted as we acknowledge that we are part of life.

9

Be Loving to Yourself

When you do nice things for yourself, you send a message of love to the Cherished Self. This helps you build a positive self-image, which in turn will generate even more loving feelings toward yourself.

Unfortunately, many of us are busy doing things mostly for others, and as a result, we tend to neglect ourselves. These others include: our bosses, our partners, our children, our family and our friends. *We constantly look for ways to give to others,* and we can actually be quite vigilant about it. We also worry about what others will think about us and, as a result, spend a lot of time pondering how we look, what we will drive, what we will wear, how we will act, and how much money we're going to make.

the cherished self

When we are preoccupied with others in these ways, we can become very inept at taking care of our own needs. Some people might say it's selfish to do nice things for yourself. But what's actually dangerous is giving so much to others that we deplete ourselves. There's great truth in the saying, "In order to love others, we must first love ourselves."

The Depleted Self or The Cherished Self?

When we take time for ourselves and make giving to ourselves a high priority, we are cherishing ourselves. Soon we begin to have a glow about us. We start to have more energy. We stop yelling at our children or partners, and we can give to others from our overflow.

Sometimes what we love to do is buried deep within us

If it has been awhile since you thought about what you enjoy doing, you may feel a little rusty at coming up with ideas. When I first encourage clients to begin cherishing themselves, many say, "I don't even know what I like to do anymore. It's been so long since I thought of doing something nice for myself."

This is a sad admission, yet it can be important because it clears the path for change. I urge my clients to begin writing a list.

I have observed that it's usually the simple things that people enjoy doing, such as a stroll in the park, having dinner with friends, listening to music, laughing, renting a funny movie, snuggling on the couch, having your hair brushed, reading a good book, lighting candles, taking a bath, flying a kite, writing a poem, baking cookies, throwing a Frisbee, walking the dog, doing ceramics, going to garage sales, or having a massage.

Be Loving to Yourself

Other ways of being nice to yourself include going out to a movie, writing a letter, rearranging the furniture, working in the garden, knitting, attending a festival, going for a drive in the country, spending time with children, exploring a museum, and relaxing at an outdoor jazz concert.

Or you might choose sports activities that you enjoy, such as golf, tennis, volleyball, swimming, aerobics, jogging, hiking, fishing, boating, rowing, sailing, climbing, or water skiing.

As you can see, the opportunities are endless. You might choose something as simple as going out for a cup of coffee, or taking a class. I encourage you to start making your own list today. *Do something nice for yourself.*

Make a list of ways to be loving to yourself

Think of the things in life that bring charm, joy and pleasure to your soul. Make an on-going list, and place it in a spot where the list will remind you to do something nice for yourself on a regular basis. Start with 50 ways to cherish yourself. Share the list with your partner or a close friend and encourage them to help you do nice things for yourself.

Set aside some time just for you. One of the greatest ways to cherish yourself is to find time for yourself. Block out time every week to do a separate special activity. Refer to your list for ideas of what you'd enjoy.

the cherished self

On being receptive

We love ourselves when we can allow others to give to us. I once had a friend who was constantly doing for others. It was exhausting just watching her!

One day I said, "Please let me give to you for once. Try and receive my gift of wanting to do something nice for you." She looked sad and said, "I don't know how to allow people to give to me, it makes me feel uncomfortable." I smiled and responded encouragingly, "Just give it a try and maybe you'll feel how good it is to be loved."

Over time, my friend learned to allow others to give to her. My friend's life changed and she didn't have to be so strong and in control all the time. Her walls began to come down.

I watched my friend blossom. She opened up and allowed an incredible man to become her husband. She reduced her client load and began to spend quality time with friends. Most important, she allowed herself to feel loved.

A few years later, her brother was diagnosed with cancer. My friend went to be by his side through a period of chemo treatments.

She recognized that he was not able to receive her love and support. She told him, "Give me the pleasure of giving to you. Let go of having to take care of me and allow me to love and support you."

Later after his recovery, he saw me and said that her message had changed his life. He had learned the value of receiving love. He said, "I only knew how to be strong and to be there for everyone else. Now I have experienced what love *feels* like."

Appreciate beauty

Here's one more way that you can be loving to yourself . . . learn to appreciate beauty in its many forms. Since the Cherished Self is always expanding its horizons, you can continue to discover beauty in new places. In art, music, food, dance and other aspects of culture. Relishing the idea of surrounding ourselves with beauty delights the soul.

Surrounding ourselves in beauty doesn't mean that we have to spend a fortune. Beauty is everywhere. You might add fresh flowers to the living room, clean the windows to let the sunshine in, or place a painting or photograph on a wall you frequently walk past. By increasing your awareness and making a conscious effort, turn up the beauty in your world.

To help us appreciate beauty, we must first recognize its value. Learning to see beauty as diversity opens up a whole new perspective for us; we can then recognize that every human face has beauty and a unique story to tell. Beauty comes in all shapes, sizes and colors. Beauty is a part of all cultures. Seeing the beauty in diversity allows us to behold the gifts within all things. We can then approach life with a new perspective; open up and behold.

When we learn to appreciate beauty in all things, we can learn to appreciate and accept our own beauty. Within each of us, there is beauty to behold. Seeing our own beauty may feel egotistical and awkward if we stopped to look at our own magnificence. But when we cherish ourself, we see our own beauty and rejoice in the charm and grace of our essence.

the cherished self

To learn to appreciate your own beauty, start by making a list of the attractive things you notice in yourself. The list may include things from any and all aspects of your life such as your smile, your eyes, your hair, your personality, your laugh, your style, your intelligence, your grace, your devotion, your creativity, your humor, your talent, your adventuresomeness, your legs, your toes, your hobbies, your compassion, your acceptance, your peace, your willingness, your freedom, or your sparkle. Keep the list handy and look at it often. Read it outloud and rest in the comfort of who you are . . . *a beautiful shining being.*

Delight the senses

It's important to delight the senses daily. We have the ability to smell, to see, to taste, to touch, and to hear. When we are cherishing ourself, we are delving into the many ways to delight our senses. Unfortunately, many of us rush through our days, numb to the pleasure of our senses.

Oh the variety of ways to please our sense of taste! Yet we have become frequent consumers of fast food, eating in our cars, barely finding time to eat, let alone slowing down to appreciate the flavors and sensation of different foods.

And how underappreciated the sense of smell is! This is despite the fact that aromas can ignite memories, healing and relaxation. Learning to incorporate aromas into our day brings us a refreshing hint of comfort.

Touch. Sadly, in many lives, the warmth of a gentle touch has been replaced with distance and loneliness. There's nothing as nurturing as the feeling of a well-meaning hug or gentle pat on the back. Touch can and does heal. When we are cherishing ourself, it is important to be touched, held and nurtured. Schedule a massage, ask for a hug, or hold your partner's hand.

To see. The sense of sight is one of our most incredible senses. Give your eyes a treat and look for beauty. Surround yourself with beautiful things. Notice what is pleasing to your eye, and then indulge your sense of sight by staying on the lookout for beauty.

Turn up your sense of hearing. Play delightful music, instigate a compelling conversation, or listen for a child's laughter or a baby's giggle. Learn to speak in gentle ways and listen for the gifts in conversation.

Sometimes I like to take it a step further and think of ways to delight all my senses at once. I will decorate the house with fresh flowers, light aromatherapy candles, take a bubble bath, and play soothing music. I then put on a beautiful and comfortable robe and drink some delicate tea out of my favorite mug. I light a fire and curl up with a good book. Sometimes I even have a few Oreo cookies and a glass of milk to top off the evening.

Delight the senses

Set aside a day or an evening to delight all five senses. Design a plan of the sensations you want to create and then bring this experience to life. Give each sensation respect and appreciation. Write about your experience in your journal.

10

Painful Times Polish Us

We all walk through emotionally painful periods in our lives. In the midst of all the discomfort, there are gifts of personal growth to discover. *When you keep your attention on the gifts, you come through the fire polished.*

Many of us feel betrayed and controlled by the negative circumstances we experience. And it's common to hold onto resentments from the past. If we insist on seeing ourselves as victims in these ways, our inner spirit will begin to perish.

Pain as a companion

I propose that you begin to view emotional pain as a helpful companion. At first this suggestion may seem odd to you. The truth is that I do not wish painful times on any of us. Yet pain is a part of life. I believe that changing your perspective on pain will help you get past it.

So the next time you are confronted with difficult circumstances, try looking at pain in this way. *Your companion is telling you that this is a time to feel and grow.* For it is during difficult periods that we are forced to discover or recover an inner part of ourselves.

Often these painful or difficult challenges appear in our lives when we are ready to grow but are resisting the step forward. So our companion, pain, gives us a push to move ahead. If we keep resisting, the pain will continue. Maybe we are clinging to the security of a job we dislike or a relationship that holds us back. In some way, we are ignoring our soul's desires. Still our companion, pain, persistently calls out for our attention.

Sometimes painful circumstances are extremely challenging and feel cruelly unfair. But if we insist on being stuck in our pain without any action to move beyond it and learn from it, then our only reward will be more pain.

Pain does not lie

A minister once said to me, "Pain does not lie. *Pain is a true friend because it will always reveal to you what you need to see, feel or address.*"

Pain is like that friend who loves you so much that they tell you the truth even though they know it will hurt. And it tells you what you need to hear. Even so we may delay facing the truth in our life because we are scared and don't think we have the courage, strength or resources to survive.

But still pain does not lie. Pain sees through all your *layers* and is there to coerce you into growing.

Pain directs our attention

Pain often appears when we are neglecting our inner self and our mission in life. At these times, pain will present itself to tell us where we need to direct our attention. And if we don't respond, it will soon begin to hurt so deeply that we are forced to look within and discover the true problem.

At other times, the intense pain comes on abruptly. I mentioned earlier that when a job I held in the film industry ended suddenly, I felt lost. I thought my world had been pulled out from beneath me. I also felt hurt, scared, betrayed and alone.

These were not comfortable feelings but I needed to recognize and own the pain. I needed to feel to get to the core of it. My soul had to plunge to a great depth for me to finally recognize the gifts of the situation.

Then when I emerged from the pain, I was renewed. Eventually I realized that losing my job was a gift. It forced me to see inside my soul and allowed me the opportunity to ask myself some very honest, life-altering questions. Was the price of my success worth the cost of placing myself in an unhealthy work environment? I now know that if I hadn't lost the job, I would never have discovered how to cherish myself. It was time for me to follow my soul's purpose and realize that the pain directed me there.

the cherished self

When you create a readiness within yourself to embrace the painful circumstances in your life and look for the gifts, you are truly cherishing yourself.

Turning pain into progress

Individuals who use pain to grow are inspirations to all of us. Many leaders have been propelled by extraordinarily painful experiences, and great organizations have sprung up because of painful problems in society that need to be addressed.

Here are some examples.

Organizations:
- Mothers Against Drunk Driving (MADD)
- Domestic violence support groups
- The National Association for the Advancement of Colored People (NAACP)
- The Museum of Tolerance, Los Angeles
- The Nature Conservancy and other environmental groups
- Alcoholics Anonymous

People
- Helen Keller
- Martin Luther King, Jr.
- Oprah Winfrey
- Franklin D. Roosevelt
- Nelson Mandela
- Ghandi
- Mother Theresa
- Joan of Arc

Now write down some other people or organizations who have risen above tragedy to find their gifts.

The cherished self keeps watch, makes friends with pain, and looks for the gifts

When you are cherishing yourself, you are in tune with your life. You listen for the subtle messages that it is trying to tell you. Sometimes you can avoid a trauma or a crisis in life by listening to your inner self and trusting your intuition. Because of this, you're likely to have fewer painful times when you are cherishing yourself.

When you do have pain, look lovingly at the situation, take very good care of yourself, seek support, and look for the lessons. Be patient with yourself. Be very gentle with yourself. You'll need extra nurturing, time alone, and time to grieve.

Let the pain out so you can feel it and uncover what's underneath. Pain can hurt to the core. Be willing to feel the pain. Let yourself cry, be depressed, or withdraw. Gifts are about to be revealed. What they are may not be apparent right away, but give it time. Keep your attention on the gifts.

Even tragic circumstances can reveal gifts

Some tragic events in our lives make no sense. It is as if we are the unfortunate holders of the selected ticket in a terrible lottery. Yet *even the most horrific of experiences can bring the gift of growth along with the pain.*

I have a dear friend who was brutally raped in a dark alley one night after work. She had just stepped off the bus and was attacked as she walked home. Years later she told me, "I never want to go through that experience or anything remotely like it. Yet I have to say that it woke me up." She took charge of her life after that experience. She made a number of positive changes and today she is happy.

the cherished self

Another dear friend lost both her parents due to illness when she was just a young girl. She might have allowed that situation to dampen her spirit throughout her life. Yet she hasn't. She courageously faced her pain and is a living inspiration to all her friends, clients and relatives.

The gifts

What are some of the gifts that you are able to identify today that resulted from painful times in the past?

Examples

- The end of a marriage brings self-discovery and eventually a healthier relationship.

- Downsizing and the loss of a job results in a new, more fulfilling career

- A disappointing date prompts lessons in relating

Write down at least five examples from your own life.

An invitation to allow a new friend into your life

I invite you to allow your pain to be your companion and trusted friend in life. I realize painful times are never easy, welcomed or encouraged, yet we all face them. When you embrace the idea that this experience has within it a unique gift just for you then you are sure to gain a greater awareness of who you are. You unconsciously will develop an inner strength to assist you through the painful journey.

11

The Elegance of Simplicity

Simplicity is being centered in self so that you are able to recognize the sacred moments in the ordinary occurrences of life. Simplicity is merely the outcome of "beingness." To *be* with oneself is to connect with the wonder of who you are and realize you are more than enough just the way you are. Simplicity is being authentic.

Simplicity reconnects us to ourselves

To create simplicity in life, you have to connect with your true self. Most of us live in constant perpetual motion. We have external obligations as well as constant mind chatter, society's expectations, our personal drive to compete, and our sense of longing to be loved that act as decoys preventing us from connecting with our inner self.

But even letting go of clutter, slowing down, or moving to the country to get away from constant external forces will not in and of itself allow us to experience simplicity.

Simplicity requires a personal decision that you are enough just the way you are. It is an outcome of cherishing yourself and discovering your authentic self.

When I began to cherish myself, my life became less cluttered with the constant motion of activity. It was then that I could deepen my connection with myself. I was able to tap into the core of my humanness and experience the beauty and grace of every moment. I call this *simple elegance.*

Simplicity is balance

When you are being authentic, your life is in balance. Balance is a customized fit for each individual. For me, balance meant slowing down, leaving my demanding career, and following my heart. For others, balance may mean stepping into more activity yet still finding time to be still and be centered. *Simplicity is to strike a delicate balance between stimuli and stillness.*

To be balanced is to strive for the center of your being. We can all be in life and be centered and balanced. When you live a balanced life, you find yourself in the middle of opposites. Balance does not mean boring, stale or plain. It also does not mean continual excitement and drama.

If you have constant boredom, lack of challenge, or a sense of numbness, you will eventually become disinterested in life. If you experience perpetual excitement and drama, you will eventually be depleted.

Elegance of Simplicity

There is a balance. When you strive for this balance in life, you are cherishing yourself and life is simplified.

Define your balance

Are you constantly in motion? If so, write down all the activities that distract you from being in touch with yourself.

Or are you bored with life? Do you wish you had more to do? What pastimes could you add to your life that would be true to who you are?

Are you already in balance? If this is true for you, congratulations! It's time to acknowledge the ways you manage your life so that you are not overburdened. Write your strategies down. These notes can serve as a reminder at a time when you find it to be more of a challenge to maintain balance.

Simplicity is an inner attitude

When you choose a cherished life, you begin to naturally dissolve your compulsive nature to acquire possessions, generate constant mind chatter, and do never-ending tasks. Authenticity breeds simplicity of life. Simplicity allows you to be centered to deal with life's twists and turns.

I have realized that a mark of simplicity is a certain attitude towards life's upsets. It involves being aware of your reactions. Life will always present disappointments. You will make mistakes throughout time, you will be late occasionally, crises will surface. However you have a choice about how you are affected.

the cherished self

If you choose to simplify your life, then you could be in the midst of a huge project and still feel at peace. You could be behind with a deadline, and still experience simplicity.

Being connected to ourself allows us to react to life from a centered place. A simplified life means we stop and consider our reaction to life's upsets. We recognize when we are responsible for triggering a burst of activity based on our reaction. We know that every action creates more action. When we are centered, we respond to life's challenges from a place of inner wisdom. We steer clear of drama for the sake of drama.

To live simply is to stay connected to self even in the height of stressful situations, crisis and unexpected occurrences. You are responsible for the level of activity in your life. Perpetual activity is a detour away from tapping into your sacred space.

Ways to discover simplicity in everyday life

Let go of the need to be in motion
Most of us have an attachment to the activities of our lives. We feel in some way measured by our level of activity and see ourselves as more important when we have more to do. Simplicity is knowing we are enough just the way we are.

Go into the silence
Connect with your inner self. True simplicity is created when we are living an authentic life. When we go into the silence, we tap into our inner selves and stay true to our path home.

Learn to say "no"
Simplicity is knowing how to say "no" from a place of inner wisdom.

Clear out the clutter of your life
There are all kinds of clutter in your life. There is material clutter like the piles of "stuff" on your desk, in your closet, in your junk drawer, or scattered around your garage. When you clear out the material clutter, your life magically opens up with possibility.

There is also "mind clutter." Mind clutter is the internal chatter that fills your head and takes your precious energy. Be mindful of your thoughts and allow only those thoughts that are nurturing and true to who you are.

Live authentically
Only you know what your authentic life is. You may need to leave that job, move to the country, or resign from the association. When you live authentically, you create a simplified life.

Less really is more
Society pushes us to believe more is better. When we believe that grander is better, we lose sight of the sacred in the ordinary moments of life.

Now that I am cherishing myself, I would rather enjoy a simple picnic than go to a fancy restaurant. I would choose to go to a garage sale over a department store. I'd rather send a card than make a phone call. I prefer having dinner with pals over going to a night club. I would rather help a friend than complete the next errand. And I'd pick gazing at a sunset over watching TV.

Simplicity also meant wanting to experience the feeling I felt growing up in a small Nebraska town. Experiencing a sense of connectedness to the community, rather than be lost in an urban track.

the cherished self

I believe such simplicity gives us a higher quality of life. These days, I am more in touch with the people in my life as well as the natural world. And the act of slowing down and turning to my own thoughts gives me a stronger connection to myself. These gifts are grander than any amount of power, prestige or possession. *Life is simply elegant.*

Appreciate the beauty along the way

When life is simplified, you see more beauty in the world. You notice a child's smile, connect with nature, and see the subtle color in your partner's eyes.

When your days are cluttered with the constant whirl of activity, you miss these things and more. Is that living?

It's time to discover the joys of simplicity.

12

When You Slip Off the Path

Deciding to cherish yourself is not a one-time decision. As your life pulls at you from many directions, you'll find yourself tempted occasionally to give up on cherishing yourself. At those moments, you'll need to reaffirm your commitment to your Cherished Self.

But no matter how hard you try, there's bound to be periods when you actually slip off the path of cherishing yourself for awhile. It could be for a few hours, a day, a week, or even several months.

It may be that you've fallen back into the pattern of saying yes to requests that you really want to turn down. Even though you don't have the time, you've agreed to be on yet another committee, to have a social gathering at your house, to watch a friend's children, or to take on another project. You notice that you've begun to push yourself and have less time for journaling or for entering the silence.

And before you know it, you don't remember the last time you had a quiet moment for yourself, took a peaceful walk, wrote down your thoughts and feelings, or did something nice just for you.

Stress & the cherished self

When you're under stress, you want to be sure that you do not abandon the tools you use to cherish yourself. In fact, that's just when you need them the most.

When your life is putting increasing pressure on you to do more and more, reach out to the Steps of the Cherished Self. They will help support you through those demanding times. Observe your life, go into the silence, journal your feelings, use your imagination, rely on your enhancing relationships, be loving to yourself, connect with nature, and trust your life process. *Using the tools will keep you committed to taking care of yourself and keep you in balance when things around you are out of control.*

I find in my own life, if I take the time to cherish myself, I can actually do more, will be more at peace, will have more creative energy, will be more available as a loving partner, and will laugh more. For instance, when I take the time to quiet my mind before a lecture, I find I connect better with my audience. If I journal when stress is giving me the blues, I can uncover the cause of my sadness and take a responsible action rather than blame someone else.

However I also occasionally slip off the path of cherishing myself. But I do this less often because I've learned an important secret. *It helps to be able to recognize when you're about to slip.*

When You Slip Off the Path

Cherished self alert

When you cherish yourself, you need to become super vigilant about your habits. You want to be aware of your own tendencies and note the signals that you're about to slip.

For example, when you're not cherishing yourself, do you tend to:

- Overwork
- Lose sleep
- Eat more
- Spend too much money

Look for such behaviors and they can become your own personal signals that you need to give yourself special attention. This is the time to kick into Cherished Self high gear. Do the steps as often as necessary.

Being able to pinpoint the signals of a pending departure helps you to be responsible for continuing to create the life of your dreams.

You know you're slipping when. . .

List your own personal signals that you are not cherishing yourself. Think of the behaviors that you know you do when you are under pressure. These will be indicators that you are slipping off the path of cherishing yourself and that you need to assess what's happening in your life.

---

the cherished self

Stress & survival mode

When you slip off the path of cherishing yourself, you may become comfortable and even adapt to the higher stress level. But often when we adapt in this way, we shift into an unconscious state regarding our own well-being. We go into survival mode.

This process starts with a feeling that you can barely keep your head above water. You feel overwhelmed and are afraid that life will engulf you if you slow down for even a few minutes. So you keep pushing forward. Soon a strange thing happens . . . you adapt to your stressful environment.

But when we continually adapt to stressful times, we place ourselves at risk for illness, accidents and emotional blockages. And the scary part is that we sometimes don't even recognize that we've slipped off the path.

After long periods of stress, we may begin to notice that we're uncomfortable even when the "busy-ness" stops. If we do get a free moment, we may be at a loss of what to do with that time. I know in my own life there have been periods when working past 6 p.m. seemed like I was really putting in a long day. And then all of a sudden I would begin to consistently come home later and later until I would start getting in around 9 every night. Eventually getting home past 9 p.m. became the norm. I would actually feel like I was not putting in a full day if I did not work at least 10 hours. Looking back now, I can see that this behavior was very unhealthy, both emotionally and physically. But when I wasn't cherishing myself, I didn't even recognize the toll my work had on my life. I see this over commitment occurring in all phases of life with mothers, professionals, college students, teenagers, as well as older adults.

When You Slip Off the Path

Get back on the path

Life is an ongoing journey and sometimes that journey is about slipping off the path. The following steps are designed to help you get back on track.

1. Recognize you've slipped.
2. Forgive yourself.
3. Pinpoint the cause without assessing blame.
4. Make a responsible choice.

Recognize you've slipped
It is very important that you have signals to alert yourself when you have slipped off the path. Be aware of your behavior and the things you do when you stop cherishing yourself. I also suggest asking a trusted friend or partner to tell you when they see you stray into unhealthy or unconscious actions and habits.

Forgive yourself
We all slip off the path. What is important is that you recognize when you do and forgive yourself. Do the best you can to talk positively to yourself. Be grateful for catching yourself now and remain optimistic.

Identify the cause without assessing blame
When you are cherishing yourself, you are not looking for ways to blame others for your situation. Instead you want to pinpoint the cause of your behavior or reaction. Examine your life and discover why you are not cherishing yourself or are feeling stressed.

Make a responsible choice
You will feel empowered and in charge of your life when you make responsible choices that place you back on the track of cherishing yourself. Even taking the step to notice you've slipped is a move in

the right direction. By not forgiving yourself for your mistakes, you show disdain for yourself. Or if you surround yourself with people who do not forgive your mistakes, then you are not loving yourself. It is time to forgive yourself, have compassion for yourself, and set yourself free.

It really is up to you

When all is said and done, it is all up to you. If you've slipped for a while, that's okay. You're the one who is in control, when you're ready to get back on track, you'll do it. I encourage you to stay in tune with yourself so you'll see yourself beginning to slip.

Applaud your tenacity for keeping yourself on the path to loving yourself. Every time you slip you are actually learning more about yourself. And every time you get back on track you are loving yourself more.

13

Compassion Opens the Door to Your Heart

One of the most heartwarming gifts of cherishing yourself is the awakening of compassion for yourself and others. The key to compassion is accepting the fullness of who you are, the good and powerful parts of yourself as well as the fragmented and vulnerable parts.

Within all of us, there is an inner convergence of our ideal self and our wounded self. Proudly we wear our accomplishments, like medals of honor, but tucked ever so deeply under the veil of our branded goodness is our wounded self. Within our wounded self, we store our tormented past filled with personal disappointments, poor judgments, forbidden thoughts and personal failures.

the cherished self

Compassion is acceptance

To accept all of yourself is to recognize you are both a person capable of creating good in life as well as recognizing that you are vulnerable to making mistakes. And so are other people. Validate and accept your humanness. Once we connect with our own imperfections, doubts and wounds, we can allow others to be vulnerable too.

Compassion is to let go of expectations of self and others. A Cherished Self knows that we are all human and prone to imperfections. You no longer expect yourself or others to be perfect. You allow yourself and others to grow in just the right way.

View your past mistakes as a resource

The fullness of who you are includes your personal history; all of your experiences and choices that have created a uniquely paved journey home to yourself. As you live, you grow and change. *The good choices as well as the mistakes have created who you are today.*

The Cherished Self has a responsibility to find the courage to accept all of who they are and to use that information as an inner resource in life. I know in my life there have been experiences from my past that I wish I could go back and erase. But the truth is that I would not be the person I am today if I hadn't walked down that path.

For example, I know I am not the young twenty-year-old who spent too much money and plunged into debt. I am not the same woman who agreed to commit to an unhealthy relationship. And I am not the same person who became consumed by her career.

But all of those experiences have combined to create who I am today.

I have learned from my past and I am now able to make better choices. I have grown, forgiven myself, and developed compassion for myself and others.

I am becoming every moment. Today I would not let myself go into debt. Today I am married to a healthy loving man. Today I choose to follow my passion and be true to myself.

Our past has guided us to this moment and our inner wisdom has charted the way. When we are able to fully accept our fragmented past, we are able to unconditionally love ourselves.

Free yourself of disempowering thoughts

Find the courage to explore the inner wounds and find the gifts. When you feel shame, guilt, embarrassment, resentment, disgust or disappointment in yourself, you contaminate the sacred space within you. These disempowering thoughts are silent saboteurs in your life.

Your negative beliefs are capable of unconsciously sabotaging the good in your life. They can even reside in your body as disease, discomfort, or perpetual disappointments. When things are about to go right in your life it is as if someone says to you, "You don't deserve to have good things happen to you. Remember you are imperfect and you don't deserve happiness."

But if you can not move beyond your mistakes, then you begin to hold yourself hostage to your past.

By not forgiving yourself for your mistakes, you show disdain for yourself. Or if you surround yourself with people who do not forgive your mistakes, then you are not loving yourself. *It is time to be forgiving and compassionate and set yourself free.*

the cherished self

Trying to be perfect pushes love away

When you don't forgive yourself for your mistakes, you are unable to love yourself fully. You create a disconnected self. You then do not believe that others will love you either. So you set yourself up to cover up your imperfect parts.

The only problem with this strategy is that it prevents someone from ever fully loving you. You always keep love at a safe distance. Additionally, you then believe you have to "have it all together" to be lovable. This keeps true love out of your life.

When I began to cherish myself, I began to love and accept all parts of myself. I wanted to disown some of my decisions of the past but I knew I needed to love myself unconditionally. This meant I needed to embrace my mistakes and realize the many blessings from them.

I am not suggesting that you have to broadcast your soul's shadow side to every person or even to anyone other than yourself; what I'm saying is that it's an inside job. Only you can forgive yourself and see yourself as whole, perfect and complete.

I was personally terrified of sharing my less than perfect past with my partner. When I began to disclose things to him, I discovered he had the capacity to love me even more.

This was one of the greatest experiences of my life. I was so afraid of being unlovable. Then I experienced unconditional love.

Let go of judgments

It is a human tendency to judge everyone, including ourself, but judgments are like venom. I believe we project a dangerous poison on the lives of others and ourselves when we judge. And other people project the same type of venom on us with their judgments. *This is cruel.*

When we have compassion, we do not judge others by such things as their economic status, their body, their disease, their nationality, their job, their dress or their past. We also do not judge ourselves.

We could all use more compassion. If we felt more compassion in life, we would feel safer and be more willing to be authentic.

Free yourself

Sit quietly, close your eyes, and think about your life's journey. Recognize the fullness of who you are. Acknowledge your goodness and all the contributions you make to the lives of others. Write about these contributions in your journal.

Now think about the mistakes, poor judgments, or disappointments in your life. Think back to the times when you made the mistakes. Why did you make these decisions? What was going on in your life then? How did you feel about yourself? Who were your friends? Write about yourself at the time of these mistakes.

Now think about yourself today. Have you changed? Did you learn from the mistake? Do you have compassion for others who are going through similar experiences?

Recognize the gifts that these experiences have given you. See yourself as a wise person who needed to go down the path just the way you did. Forgive yourself.

the cherished self

Compassion for others

When you have compassion, you see past the imperfect behavior of others and see their heart. When you see the heart of a person, you realize we are all pretty much the same. Each of us is human, we all have a heart, and we all make mistakes. And each of us wants to be loved.

I like to say to myself, "Their heart hurts like my heart, their heart loves like my heart, and they are just like me." Then I am able to have compassion for their mistakes.

Sometimes this can be quite a challenge. It's especially tough when you encounter a difficult person, someone who grinds your nerves, someone who is acting inappropriate, or someone whose behavior is unhealthy.

The trick is to recognize their pain. Realize that a series of painful events have led them to this moment. Know that they are dealing with their pain the best way they know how. And their pain is the real reason that they are so righteous, angry, demanding or cruel.

At the same time, I do not believe anyone should tolerate abuse or any level of unhealthy conditions. But I do believe that we can do our best to see through to the hearts of difficult people and send these individuals compassion. The best way I know how to send compassion to a difficult person is to refrain from targeting them with negative thoughts.

Everyone could use a little more compassion. The homeless person on the street, the rich and famous, the President of the United States, and the criminal.

14

Destination Unknown

Destination Unknown is about learning how to tap into your inner wisdom and live authentically moment by moment. When you allow your inner wisdom to guide you, you step into the flow of life. Magically miracle after miracle begins to occur.

When you are not living in harmony with yourself, you feel exhausted and empty inside. Instead of tapping into your inner wisdom to guide your decisions, you look to external forces to provide the clues.

Each of us has a wise inner guide that is capable of leading us home to ourselves. To live life in the flow we need to do two things: *surrender and trust.*

the cherished self

The best way I have discovered to learn the lessons of surrender and trust is to try an unusual type of adventure . . . I call it *Destination Unknown.*

Destination unknown adventures

Years ago I stumbled into a fun and simple way to tap into my inner wisdom . . . going on outings or trips without a destination. Today Destination Unknown Adventures are a regular part of my life.

First I surrender and relinquish all planning regarding my final location. To assure a good time, I prepare for any kind of weather or circumstance. Even for a day's outing, I take along a jacket, extra casual clothes and sometimes a nice outfit, and for longer adventures, additional clothes. Then I'm off on an outing for the day or on a trip for the weekend or more, without knowing where I'm headed. I just get in the car and go! I let my free spirit guide me and take me places.

What occurs is a feeling of excitement, and as you open up to the experience, anticipation builds. Destination Unknown Adventures bring out the child in all of us. You grow more comfortable with surrender and trust.

Thoughts on surrender

A Cherished Self recognizes when it is time to let go and allow life's magic to take over. To just give up the struggles of life and allow your inner wisdom to guide you.

Usually this happens when your life feels most challenging. You've been doing your very best and you're amazed that nothing is working, so you decide to surrender. Perfect. It *is* time to surrender.

Surrender is about releasing control over our lives. We all want total control because we fear our life will fall apart if we don't have it. And yet we can get in our own way by trying to figure life out, by controlling too much, by having too many specific expectations, by planning perpetually, and most importantly, by looking to external influences to guide our choices. All of these can prevent your soul's message from penetrating your consciousness.

I'm not saying that you should let go of all control over your life. Instead I'm suggesting that you be in control of your life by following your inner wisdom.

Thoughts on trust

You need to trust your inner wisdom to guide you through life. Your inner self is giving you signals every moment. Our job is to tune into it. Then suddenly you are aware of how you feel. If you feel uncomfortable or in conflict, trust your feelings and change your course. On the other hand, if you feel safe and happy, trust that message and follow your inner choice.

Life is guiding you moment by moment. The best way to really tap into your inner wisdom is to be still.

It's also important to let go of manipulating things to go your way. Instead, trust. Then watch carefully for the wonderful things that start to occur.

My destination unknown adventures

Let me now share how I pursue a Destination Unknown adventure.

When I get in the car, the adventure begins. Each stop sign offers a choice from my inner self. Do I want to go north, south, east or west?

Then I begin following my instincts, I might visit a museum, watch a sunset, head to the forest, or maybe just drive and drive without a sense of where I'll end up.

I'm always delighted with my discoveries. Whether I meet an interesting person, discover a new hiking trail, listen to a jazz band, shop at an antique shop, or find a quaint town, I feel alive and guided.

Once I took a 12-day Destination Unknown trip. My soul knew it needed to get away for a while. I took off alone and drove through California, Nevada, Utah, Colorado, Nebraska, Kansas, Oklahoma, New Mexico and Arizona. I stopped in Nebraska and saw my family and then my mother joined me for a while. We had a special time together exploring our lives and experiencing new adventures.

I take Destination Unknown trips on a regular basis with my friends, partner and by myself.

The spontaneity and discovery of destination unknown adventures

Living life in the moment feels exhilarating! You may experience a heightened sensitivity to your surroundings. You notice different things, interesting people, and new reactions.

A playful spirit permeates from your soul. You feel spontaneous. You respond moment to moment. It feels good to risk stepping out of your routine. By allowing yourself to be spontaneous, you free your soul to be real.

When you live in the moment, you learn about your true nature. When you allow yourself to be free of outside influences, you discover what you like to do, where you like to go, and even what you notice. You tap into a greater understanding of who you are.

A friend once said to me that he loves going on Destination Unknown trips because he learns so much about himself. He said he could have gone anywhere he wanted . . . to the mountains, the ocean, a hotel or a museum. Instead he choose to go to the desert. Since he had a sleeping bag in the car, he decided to sleep outside under the stars.

He came back from his trip refreshed and redirected. He said, "I never would have guessed how much I enjoyed and needed to experience roughing it in Mother Nature."

Go on a destination unknown adventure

When was the last time you didn't plan what you would do before you went on a day outing? Or a trip away from home? You are about to experience a Destination Unknown Adventure.

First pack provisions and clothes so you can deal with weather shifts and other circumstances. Consider whether you want to travel by foot, bike, train or whatever suits your mood. Then off you go!

Experience surrender and discovery. Listen to your inner voice and allow it to guide you. What is it that you're drawn to discover?

When you return, write about your experience in your journal. Where did you go? How did it feel not to have a plan? What did you experience? Did you feel supported?

Life with a destination unknown attitude

Eventually you won't have to take a trip to experience surrender and trust. You will have the ability to tap into the attitude of Destination Unknown at all times in your life. You will be in the flow of life and know intuitively when you're off course. You can allow your inner wisdom to guide you back to what's right for you. Life will feel effortless and magical.

You will also know when you're getting in your own way and it's time to surrender. You will know how to tap into your inner wisdom. Most importantly, you will be on a guided path back to you.

Happy Destination!

Every Cherished Self
Makes a Difference!

Now that you have become a Cherished Self, you've begun the journey home to your true self. You're learning to connect to your heart. And as you get better and better at cherishing yourself, you will become more authentic, and feel more joy, fulfillment and passion.

However keep in mind that connecting internally and learning how to love yourself are not lighthearted endeavors. Instead these changes show that you have made a commitment to living a meaningful life.

the cherished self

Welcome to a meaningful life

When you are cherishing yourself, you begin to look for a deeper sense of purpose. You want your life to have meaning. And once you are in touch with your inner self, you are able to tap into your purpose. Inside each of us is a unique gift coupled with an inner desire and intention to give to the world.

You may have to dig deep into your inner self to uncover your unique gift. You do not want to assume that you have the same gift as your father, mother, neighbor, associate or friend. We all need your magnificence. What you have to offer the world is not only unmatched by anyone else, it is impossible for anyone else to be you. You are important.

Give yourself permission to be all of who you are meant to be. Let your gifts show. Follow your heart and you will not be lead astray.

My father will say to me, "You are something new in this world. Never before, since the beginning of time, has there been anybody exactly like you. Never again throughout all the ages to come will there ever be anybody like you again." He tells me often to be true to myself, and that as long as I am following my heart, he is proud of me.

He said that he didn't care what I chose to do in life as long as I loved it.

Whether you choose to sell insurance, raise children or be an actor, make sure you do it with passion and joy. Give it your all, because that is your gift to humankind.

Have you ever heard that for every problem there is a solution at hand? Yes, I believe it is true.

Every Cherished Self Makes a Difference

Yet what is required of each of us is to make our unique contribution. The world is like a human assembly line and each soul has the potential to contribute their unique part. When we are in alignment with our purpose, we tap into the miracles of life. Life supports our personal discovery to contribute our part of the plan.

You choose a cherished life simply by finding the courage and tools to be true to who you are. This does not necessarily mean you have to win the Pulitzer Prize, solve a major world problem, cure a disease, or be a world leader. Instead it's taking personal responsibility to connect with and cherish yourself.

If you have not found your life's purpose, then know that you are on the path leading you to discover it. Your entire life has been an accumulation of experiences leading you to this moment.

How to recognize your unique gift

Begin by asking yourself, "What is my purpose for this lifetime?" I believe the answer exists in the seemingly normal occurrences of your life. The answer is revealed through everyday experiences.

For example, what contribution do you make to the lives of your friends and family? What cause do you feel most passionate about? What hobbies do you enjoy? What do others always remark about you? What would you do differently if you won the lottery? If you had the money or resources to give to a cause, which one would you pick?

Look for the answer in the synchronistic events of your life. Does it seem like you always get seated next to a writer, singer or an artist? I believe these events give us clues to our true purpose.

---

the cherished self

Your life is meaningful now simply because you are alive and living. Do you know how special you are?

Find a way to give

Our world is not hopeless, though if you watch a lot of television or read the news everyday you could begin to feel desperate and doomed. But that is not the way of a Cherished Self.

Instead find a way to give. Remember you're giving from your over-flow. Your giving is an important contribution to improving our world condition.

Your ideas, efforts and donations make our world a better place. We need you. The world needs you.

Before you turn your head or become so resigned to the pain of another day . . . take a moment, reach within and find a way to make a difference.

Our potential is great: we create where our attention lies. So place your attention on the solution, focus and believe in miracles. And then, little by little you can help make the world a more loving place.

Every Cherished Self Makes a Difference

Ways to give

You may be asking questions like: "How do I start?" or "What can I do to make a difference?" I want to suggest that you begin with a list.

Write down the things that are bothering you about our world today. Next, list ways in which you may be able to help. Then begin to contact organizations in your community and learn about efforts already in existence. Or you may want to find ways to give on your own. Maybe you feel a calling to start an effort of your own. Within you is a calling: listen and then take action. *The potential is endless.*

Closing Thoughts

Celebrate life

What is left to say other than . . . Celebrate life! Have a meaningful life of love, purpose, good health and happiness. And until you take that last breath, live life to the fullest. Spread love to others. See the exquisite beauty in every individual's eyes. Keep expecting the very best. Rejoice in the ecstasies of life that are knocking at your door. Believe in miracles because you are one.

Be an ever unfolding Cherished Self. Learn new ways to be good to yourself. Follow your heart and be true to your path.

And until we meet again, I wish for you cherished thoughts.

From *the Cherished Self*

Please contact us if you'd like to know about lectures, workshops, future publications, products or would like to be on our mailing lists.

To Order Books

Yes, I want the Cherished Self.

Quantity	Item	Price	Total
_____	*the Cherished Self*	**$ 12.95**	$_____

1st book Shipping and Handling	$ _3.00_
($1.50 for each additional book)	$_____
Sales Tax (CA residents add 7.75% sales tax)	$_____
TOTAL ORDER	$_____

By Telephone: Call (888) 465-5416 with a MC or Visa

Name: _____

Address: _____

City: _____ State: _____ Zip: _____

Telephone: _____ E-mail: _____

MC/Visa #: _____ Exp: _____

Name on the card: _____

By Fax: (888) 465-5416 Send this form.

By Mail: Just fill out the information above and send with your remittance to:

The Cherished Self
31878 Del Obispo PMB #118-311
San Juan Capistrano, CA 92675

Visit us online at: www.cherishedself.com